Praise about Robert Masters' Body of Work

"Robert Masters is an explorer of not only the contemporary mind but also the mind of history and myth. His extraordinary investigations have taken him through the territories of sex and magic, psychotherapy and psychospiritual practices, psychedelics and symbology."

—Joan Halifax, Ph.D., anthropologist,
author of *The Fruitful Darkness*

"I believe that Masters actually has broken through to a new understanding of the sense and uses of the disciplines of inward-turned contemplation—an understanding that leaves the Freudian schools of technique and theory far behind."

—Joseph Campbell, author of
Hero with a Thousand Faces and *The Power of Myth*

"Pioneer of modern consciousness research."

—Stanislav Grof, author of
Psychology of the Future and *The Holotropic Mind*

"Masters has created a beautifully designed linearly developing series of programs for inducing willing participants to change . . . their usual states of consciousness."

—John C. Lilly, M.D., author of
The Mind of the Dolphin and *The Deep Self*

"Through a combination of solid scholarship, inspiration, and hands-on psychological practice, Dr. Masters has made the ancient concepts (about subtle bodies) broadly comprehensible."

—John Anthony West, Egyptologist,
author of *Serpent in the Sky*

"Masters is a brilliant explorer of human consciousness and the mind/body realm."

—*Somatics Journal*

Swimming Where Madmen Drown

Books Authored or Coauthored
By Robert Masters (R.E.L. Masters)

Swimming Where Madmen Drown

TRAVELERS' TALES FROM INNER SPACE

ROBERT MASTERS

INNER
OCEAN

Inner Ocean Publishing, Inc.
P.O. Box 1239
Makawao, Maui, HI 96768-1239

Cover design: Bill Greaves
Interior page design: Bill Greaves
Interior page typography: Madonna Gauding
Cover and interior illustrations: Darren Hopes, Debut Art
Editing: Hal Zina Bennett

Library of Congress Cataloging-in-Publication Data

Masters, Robert E.L.
      Swimming where madmen drown : travelers' tales from inner space /
   Robert Masters. - -Makawao, Maui, Hawaii : Inner Ocean, 2002.

        p. ; cm.
     ISBN 1-930722-07-9
        1. Consciousness. 2. Perception. 3.
     Reality. 4. Altered states of
     consciousness. I. Title.

BF311 .M37 2002
153 - -dc21   CIP

Printed in Canada by Friesens

9 8 7 6 5 4 3 2 1

*This book is dedicated
to the Priestesses
of Sekhmet*

Contents

Foreword

Early navigators wrote about "antipodes," remote places on the globe diametrically opposite to those already known and explored. Aldous Huxley used the phrase "antipodes of the mind" when he referred to those mental experiences that seem to be incredibly different than what most people regard as what is "true" or "real." Robert Masters is an intrepid explorer of these antipodes, and this book contains accounts of several of his exploits. Some of his adventures are so exotic and uncanny that a few of his readers may wonder how to make sense of stories that stretch the boundaries of their worldviews or deconstruct them altogether. I suspect that more than a few individuals have found themselves at these antipodes and have been unable to keep their heads above water. However, Dr. Masters has developed the dexterity to merrily swim in the same currents where madmen drown.

In my own work with extraordinary human experiences, I have utilized an evaluation system that differentiates the confidence one can give to unusual reports and observations. Firsthand observations provide a great degree of confidence regarding extraordinary experiences, and Dr. Masters' book is replete with them. One example would be the procession of "Living Goddesses" in Kathmandu, Nepal, who are so similar in appearance one might think they had been cloned. I only saw one Living Goddess when I was in Kathmandu, but was told that once her reign ended, no man would marry her for fear of suffering an untimely demise. As a result, these young women are deities one day and outcasts the next. In another account, Dr. Masters recalls the Native American legend about Geronimo and his alleged conversations with coyotes. One night during one of my visits with Rolling Thunder, an intertribal medicine man I worked with for many years, the two of us walked to the far end of his property in the Nevada desert. Suddenly, R.T. began howling and, much to my surprise, a coyote trotted up to where we were standing. R.T. started to bark, and the coyote seemed to bark back to him, as if they were having a conversation. After the coyote left us, R.T. told me that it was important to keep in touch with his coyote friends, as they would warn each other about impending danger from hunters and marauders.

Personal experiences often provide the basis for firsthand reports. In Chapter 8, Dr. Masters writes about his experiences with peyote and other mind-altering plants. The most potent plant concoction that I have ingested is an Amazon brew, known variously as yage or ayahuasca. Although the Amazonian Indians have used this drink ceremoniously for centuries, several Brazilian churches emerged in the twentieth century that now utilize it as their sacrament. I was invited to one of their services during a trip to Brazil, and we were asked to contemplate a question we would like to pose to our "plant teachers." I queried, "What would it be like to enter the mind of God?" Sometime later, as the brew took its effect, and as I sat with my eyes closed, my question was answered. I had a mental image in which I was standing in the midst of a spectacular violet tower. The walls were lined with colorful tiles, and each rectangle was inscribed with a mathematical formula. A few of the formulae were followed by asterisks, and I realized that these were the natural laws that humanity had discovered. It was a humbling experience to fathom how many tiles there were and how few asterisks! I also had the realization that the word "supernatural" is a misnomer; human beings may have any number of astonishing experiences, but they are all "lawful" and "natural," even if humanity has yet to evoke a sensible explanation or a valid formula. As Dr. Masters remarks in another chapter, after discussing so-called Tibetan thought forms, "physics will eventually render a sensible explanation."

Reports and experiences provide what the psychologist Abraham Maslow once called "a teeny bit of evidence," but misperceptions, misunderstandings, faulty memory, and outright deception can compromise their veracity. A controlled observation attempts to prevent some of these factors from distorting an observer's experience. In Chapter 14, Dr. Masters recalls his work with the actress Diane Varsi, who I had referred to him once she had told me about the imminent loss of her feet as a result of a supposedly "incurable" infection. Following her work with Dr. Masters, Diane revisited her physician, throwing her leg brace to the floor and breaking into a dance. The physician examined her, and wrote a letter attesting to "a miracle." Dr. Masters and I did not use the word "miracle" because it would imply that a natural law had been transcended; however, we shared Diane's delight in overcoming a life-threatening condition that never recurred. Diane lived another decade, and during her last visit to my office, she expressed her gratitude to Dr. Masters for extending her lifespan.

In the behavioral sciences, the controlled experiment is considered to carry the most evidential weight when extraordinary experiences are studied. As the sociologist Marcello Truzzi once wrote, paraphrasing the philosophers Hume and Laplace, "extraordinary claims demand extraordinary proof." On occasion, I have attempted to take him at his word. In Chapter 18, Dr. Masters describes the "Witches' Cradle," an ingenious device for altering human consciousness and evoking unusual experiences. For ten years, I conducted parapsychological research at Maimonides Medical Center in Brooklyn, New York. Dr. Masters and his wife, Jean Houston, lent us a "Witches' Cradle" for an experiment in which we asked volunteers to describe their mental imagery while strapped into the cradle. They knew that a staff member was focusing on an art print in a distant room, and attempted to "journey" to that room and identify the art print. Our results were statistically significant; the more profound the alteration of consciousness, the closer the mental imagery matched the contents of the art print.

As the readers of this book work their way through Dr. Masters' accounts, they can use the following guidelines to enhance their enjoyment of the text. They can ask themselves whether some of the secondhand stories could be the result of faulty memory. Could certain of the firsthand reports be explained by an incomplete perception of the event? I often find it useful to ask myself, "If I were seeing a stage magician, how would I react to what I have just seen?" Magicians depend upon distractions, misdirections of attention, and optical illusions to create their effects. And not all clever magicians are confined to the stage! In Chapter 30, Dr. Masters admits that some of his travelers' tales were "only heard, not personally witnessed" and that he "cannot vouch for their authenticity." His readers should approach these accounts with the same degree of healthy skepticism. I would echo Marcello Truzzi's advice to distinguish between extraordinary claims that are *suggestive* (the evidence is worthy of attention but of low priority), *compelling* (the evidence is strongly supportive, arguing for a higher priority), and *convincing* (there is a preponderance of evidence supporting the claim).

At the same time, my colleagues and I have designed controlled observations and controlled experiments to study some of the same phenomena described in this book. We have recorded the psychophysiology of a Brazilian "psychic sensitive" who purports to serve as a "channel" for the spirits of dead artists to continue painting and drawing. We used psychophysiological monitoring devices to collect the dreams of an English "psychic sensitive" who was apparently able to dream about an event that took place the following day. We even designed an experiment involving synchronicity as revealed in tossing coins to consult the *I Ching,* a centuries-old Chinese book of wisdom.

In the introduction to this remarkable series of essays, Dr. Masters cites William James, the first notable American psychologist, whose cautionary statement about prematurely "closing our accounts with reality" still stands. James had explored the antipodes of the mind, and Dr. Masters has continued in this exploratory tradition. This book of travelers' tales will acquaint and delight his readers with some of the fruits of this spirited search.

Stanley Krippner, Ph.D.
Alan W. Watts Professor of Psychology
Saybrook Graduate School and Research Center
San Francisco, California

References

Cardena, E., Lynn, S.J., & Krippner, S. (Eds.). (2000). *Varieties of anomalous experience: Examining the scientific evidence*. Washington, DC: American Psychological Association.

Honorton, C., Drucker, S.A., & Hermon, H. (1973). Shifts in subjective state and ESP under conditions of partial sensory deprivation: A preliminary study. *Journal of the American Society for Psychical Research, 67,* 191-196.

Krippner, S., Ullman, M., & Honorton, C. (1971). A precognitive dream study with a single subject. *Journal of the American Society for Psychical Research, 6*, 192-203.

Rubin, L., & Honorton, C. (1971). Separating the yins from the yangs: An experiment with the *I Ching. Journal of Parapsychology, 35*, 313-314.

Truzzi, M. (1998). Unfairness and the unknown. *The Fringe, 2*, 147-152.

Acknowledgments

There are many who have shared with me one or more of the adventures mentioned in this book, and others who have contributed in a variety of important ways to the explorations and research projects here described. I especially want to give thanks to the following:

Arthur Ceppos, John Lilly, Don Snyder, Burgess Meredith, Michele Carrier, Converse Sheets, Burt Kleiner, Doris Duke, Reed Erickson, Barbara Moore, Kat Cameron, Althea Orr, Sahara, Margaret Mead, Moshe Feldenkrais—the list could be extended on and on, and I will acknowledge some others on another occasion.

Also very helpful to me in laying the groundwork for this project were my mastiffs—Titan, Queen Zingua and Captain Sir Richard Francis Burton—to whom I told travelers' tales late at night on innumerable occasions when the fire was burning in the huge fireplace and glasses of calvados or armagnac helped to bring up the memories and facilitate the telling of the tales.

Even so, this book might never have come into existence had I not enjoyed a unique creative interaction with a muse extraordinaire, Jill (aka Jewel) Bittinger. Jill's unwavering attention and interest in the process produced an effortless and almost involuntary flowing forth of words as I recalled images, sensations, emotions and other elements of what would finally emerge as the book now before you. Jill, it now is time for the next one!

As always, I acknowledge as a special gift to me from the Gods, my beloved wife, Jean. We have shared much, including a long, intense search for the knowledge and understanding of, as well as means of effecting, the actualization of human potentials that is a main theme of this book.

Finally, the coming to physical fruition of the book is indebted to various ideas about organization and contents helpfully provided by editor Hal Zina Bennett and editorial director John Nelson.

Introduction

There used to be a variety of literature sometimes called *Travelers'*
Tales. These were writings of travelers and explorers, describing
flora and fauna and peoples and behaviors quite unfamiliar and
strange to the reader. Those were times when most people stayed
close to home and it was rare that they ever left their towns or
villages and the areas nearby. Exceedingly rare were those who had
gone to strange lands where the people and customs were strik-
ingly different from their own, or into wild places harboring creatures formerly unheard of.

As often as not, there was no way to know if the "travelers'
tales" were true, or were just tantalizing fictions invented by the
tellers of the tales. In some cases, long periods of time would have
to pass before travel to such regions became common enough that
the stories could be confirmed, or possibly rejected for lack of supporting evidence.

Now our world has become one where not many places

remain inaccessible, and almost everything on earth has been filmed, videotaped, or otherwise brought within reach of anyone who is curious. As a result, travelers' tales have largely ceased to be told. Even Outer Space has been approached in such a way that rather few people any longer think of that territory as being particularly marvelous or intriguing.

For now, it would seem that only Inner Space remains as fertile ground for tales about wondrous places, alien beings of all sorts, and Powers and Principalities remaining largely uncharted and but feebly described. Inner Space is a territory of indescribable vastness, a whole universe of experience that lies far beyond the present reality consensus forged by brains and minds with potentials only slightly used as we have evolved for a brief period of time within the space of our little planet.

The book you are holding contains many examples of experiences that challenge our present understandings of reality and that involve in one way or another aspects and elements of Inner Space. These are the *Travelers' Tales* of today. Like the older variety, they will, in some cases, be verified or disclaimed by future travelers. For now, they awaken a sense of wonder, causing us to reach beyond the known and the knowable.

In varying degrees we are, all of us, Inner Space travelers. In our dreams while sleeping we go sometimes to worlds unknown to us otherwise, and our bodies in dreams are not necessarily the same as our bodies when awake. There are also, for many, vivid daydreams that overwhelm and replace, for a time, the normal reality. There are states experienced when ill that remove us from that normal reality. Some people spontaneously move in and out of trances of varying depths, not always knowing what is happening to them. Everything from prolonged massage to prolonged sex, or prolonged concentration on, or absorption in, almost any activity, will alter consciousness and provide experiences not normally accessible. However, except for extreme cases, the reality consensus allows for those sorts of deviations and takes little notice of them. It is deviations that threaten in some way the consensus, the accord about what is real, the accepted understandings of cause and effect, and beliefs about human capabilities—those are the aspects of Inner Space described in these travelers' tales.

There are experiences and capacities that are considered normal and a part of the consensus in some times and places, but not so in others. Alcohol intoxication is one example. The person who is high, or drunk, on alcohol is not presently thought of as having stepped outside the norms of reality. Drug experiences, too, are fast coming to be brought into the consensus as comparable to alcohol intoxication. In the past, however, when alcohol was used with different expectations, and for different purposes, it could provide entry to the presence of Gods. These divine intoxications gave access to paranormal powers, such as prophecy and other knowledge not available apart from the intoxication. According to the ancient Greek historian Herodotus, the ancient Persians, when faced with making decisions of importance, considered each problem from two perspectives: they looked at it sober, and they looked at it drunk, and then took the best from both states in making their decision. If a matter was important, it was too important to be left to only ordinary consciousness. Evidently alcohol was the intoxicant, but it was used quite differently than we use it today, and their drunkenness, some of it when dedicated to special purposes, was not the same as present-day versions. It was, or could be, a portal to Inner Space. That potential is undoubtedly still there if we want to avail ourselves of it.

The great American psychologist William James, in his classic book *The Varieties of Religious Experience*, cautioned against any premature closing of our accounts with reality. Our normal waking consciousness, he wrote, is only one special type of consciousness, while separated from it "by only the filmiest of screens" are many other potential forms of consciousness entirely different. Apply the requisite stimulus, he said, and there they are. They are "definite types of mentality," and have their own areas of application. Those definite types of mentality, as James called them, provide access to worlds and abilities that still belong to Inner Space, but at least some of which eventually will be a part of the reality consensus. That consensus is not stable, but is added to and subtracted from, as time goes by.

There are those persons whose everyday worlds are partly within the consensus, partly outside it. Persons who are naturally gifted, or cursed, with paranormal abilities, and those diagnosed as mad, are examples. There are also those who have acquired the ability to live at the same time in different realities by means of prolonged dedication to spiritual disciplines. In this last category, some regarded as saints might be included. None of these kinds of people have any choice about being in two worlds. It is naturally, or has become, their way of being, and often is immutable.

There are also those, like myself, who have decided to *explore* Inner Space. Such an explorer is akin to an astronaut exploring

Outer Space. He or she will journey there, but with the intention of returning to the normal reality, the consensus. As with the work of the astronaut, there are hazards—most importantly, the possibility of being unable to return. But the intention is to remain fully able to exist and function sufficiently well within the normal or earthly reality.

My interest in such exploration arose out of the recognition that, as a psychologist, I was getting only warped fragments of an understanding of the mind-body system and human potentials. Such a spiritual Teacher as G. I. Gurdjieff, for example, offered a far more profound and comprehensive psychology than any contemporary psychologist, psychiatrist or psychoanalyst. The psychology of Freud, alongside that of Gurdjieff, seemed mainly to shrink and pathologize. It tended to draw everyone within a framework of psychopathology, while Gurdjieff's work pointed towards making possible what he called *human beings not in quotation marks*. Among the analysts, Carl Jung and Wilhelm Reich offered larger views of psyche and soul, but they still could not take into adequate account the realities of Inner Space and human potentials. The Magical Renaissance, effected mainly by the eccentric genius of Aleister Crowley, brought back into consideration, and the need for exploration, Inner Space realms that had been almost banished from human consciousness. Psychedelic experience opened up Inner Space with a force that simply swept away the B. F. Skinners whose rat-inspired behaviorism had dominated psychology for much too long.

My work has been kept as scientific as it can be in such areas as those where I have mainly worked—sexology, psychedelic research, hypnotic and other trance research, psychotherapy, and neural and sensory reeducation—but it has also included explorations into some of the farther reaches of Inner Space where by no current definition is the work scientific. In that connection, I have especially tried to re-create a system of ancient Egyptian magic associated with the Goddess Sekhmet and the Gods Ptah and Nefer-tem: the Triad of Memphis. There have been other explorations just to determine, so to speak, some more of what is out there. This book of travelers' tales has to do, in its way, with some of that exploring, my own and that of others.

Keep in mind that no permission is needed for such adventures. Anyone can go and do likewise.

Chapter One

Sensory and Supersensory Organs

The Sufis, some of whom are among the most advanced of all now having access to the more remote, subtle and powerful Inner Space regions, speak of fantasy, "that cornerstone of fools," and of "cognitive imagination." The unduly harsh first reference is to the ordinary imagination of a person. The second reference is to a faculty by means of which the worlds that lie beyond the reach of the ordinary senses may be known with all the fullness of the being of a person. This is where the Gods are and, at one place or another along the continuum of consciousness, all of the other Powers and Principalities lying outside of the "reality consensus."

From the earliest times, the religions and spiritual traditions have insisted on the reality of worlds beyond the everyday world, and have described the human being as possessing a number of "subtle bodies" for experiencing those worlds. The human being is always said to have a gross material body and other more subtle bodies with which to sense and to be able to function in the more subtle and also "higher" worlds. It is the task of most esoteric Schools and other psychospiritual systems to enable a person to gain awareness of, and to be able to use, these more subtle and higher bodies.

In my efforts to re-create the ancient Egyptian magic of the Triad of Memphis (Ptah, Sekhmet and Nefer-tem), I have made a prolonged and thorough study of subtle bodies, and most particularly the Way of the Five Bodies of the Goddess Sekhmet. I have written about this in my book *The Goddess Sekhmet*, and have enabled some students to gain awareness of subtle bodies and to function with respect to them. To a lesser extent, I have also explored subtle body phenomena in the magico-religious Ways of the Goddess Kali and the Hawaiian Goddess Kapo. There is no real School where such Work is not done.

Virtually all of the great sages of humanity have agreed on the reality of other worlds and intelligent nonhuman beings who populate them. Goethe, for example, who was said by his contemporaries to exemplify better than anyone else the actualized human, spoke of the spiritual eyes and ears and other spiritual senses we possess. Those who fail to learn to use those senses are blind and deaf and otherwise closed off to meaningful experience in all of the many existing worlds except for the most densely material and transient one, that of everyday reality.

To the countless human beings who have experienced the higher worlds it is evident that these worlds could not possibly be the products of their imaginations, but rather are experienced as being more real than the everyday reality. As Aldous Huxley once said, when a person first experiences these other worlds it is not as if they were somehow imagined, but rather the veil has been lifted so that one is able to see what always has been there.

Beyond the everyday world, there are hierarchies—if you will—of worlds, ranging from the less to the more subtle, from the lower to the higher, or however one should put it. Qualities of these worlds such as color and light differ from one world to the next, as do experiences of duration and of the "eternally existing" as compared to the more fleeting.

It is only in the everyday world that time moves so quickly and the duration of things, human life included, is so short. One can, in fact, return to some of the Inner Space worlds again and again, over the course of most of one's lifetime, and nothing will ever seem to have grown older, to have decayed, or to have died. It is not that there is no change in those worlds, but it is rather that we live our lives so quickly as to have no time to observe it. It is as if, for example, some kind of being like ourselves had a life span of only a few minutes, or even seconds. Then, if that being were to visit our world, she or he would not observe such processes as aging and the transiency of material forms either.

It is the proper business of every human being to go beyond that everyday world which calls for the use of just so small a part of what we are. As we come to know ourselves better, and more largely, then we gain access to senses we possess, but which were unknown to us before. A vastly larger reality opens, and we begin to awaken from the somnambulistic—or sleepwalking—state that philosophers and Teachers of humanity have always told us is the fate of everyone who remains trapped in the lower regions of existence by the crippling reality consensus prevailing in their particular place and time.

Chapter Two

Being Invisible and Being Unseen

In many magical and shamanistic traditions, there are techniques by means of which the magician or shaman becomes, in some way, invisible.

Popular books and legends often give the impression that invisibility is achieved by dematerialization. Actually, there are few serious traditions that hold that a true dematerialization ever occurs. To dematerialize the body it would have to pass out of existence so that there would be no foundation for rematerialization later on.

The magician is able to become invisible, if at all, only after very prolonged training. The techniques by which he achieves this are highly secret ones, and if described would not in any case be useful to a person who has not received the necessary training. There are, however, much more readily accessible means of becoming, for most practical purposes, invisible or, perhaps more accurately, of being unseen.

The distinction between being invisible and being unseen is essentially this: that to be invisible implies some degree of transmutation of the physical body, especially in what would appear to be a radical change in the condition of the gross material body. That body can be hidden from view by what magicians refer to as an "extrusion of subtle bodies" that then surrounds and conceals it. To be unseen, however, requires no such radical change in the magician's gross material body, although it does require some significant changes in the functioning of its nervous system.

That it is possible for a person to become invisible or to be unseen by another person is easy to demonstrate by means of certain simple hypnotic procedures. I have in mind the phenomenon known to at least some hypnotists as "negative hallucination." Most people are familiar with the idea of a "positive hallucination," or just "hallucination," meaning that the hallucinating person sees or otherwise senses something that is not physically present. In the case of the negative hallucination, the person does not see, or otherwise sense, what is physically present. It is about as easy to create one of these types of hallucination as it is to create the other. A true magician or shaman, let it be known, is always, among other things, a master hypnotist.

To illustrate negative hallucination, let us say that my assistant and I are sitting in a room conversing with a patient who is in a deep trance. I ask the person to close her eyes for a moment and then I say to her that when she opens her eyes, she will just observe that she and I are in the room. When she then opens her eyes, my assistant will have disappeared. My assistant will be unseen because I have said to the patient that she will observe that *just* she and I are in the room, and the patient will interpret that to mean that only she and I are in the room. And since only she and I are in the room, she will be unable to see my assistant or to otherwise perceive her.

By similar, or slightly more complicated, means, I myself can be negatively hallucinated by the patient or research subject and so vanish. Similarly, through direct or veiled suggestions I can take on almost any appearance I choose (positive hallucination), becoming an animal, for example, or a child; or aging, or growing younger a few years at a time, or very quickly, decades at a time, before the patient's eyes.

The magician, as a master hypnotist, can covertly induce trances and give effective suggestions to people who will then experience whatever is suggested. It is more rare, but not at all unknown, that such a hypnotist can covertly induce deep trances in even large numbers of people, becoming invisible to them, or becoming unseen.

Not long before World War II, a Russian hypnotist demonstrated that he could walk into a bank, hypnotize a teller, who would then give him a large sum of money, and walk out unseen by the guard or anyone else in the bank. This demonstration was of great interest to the Soviet Union's dictator, Josef Stalin, who was always fearful of being assassinated in the Kremlin by someone who had managed to penetrate its elaborate defenses. Stalin challenged the hypnotist who, despite the most extreme precautions, did manage to enter the Kremlin, pass by many different guards, and then appear in Stalin's own office without anyone later having any recollection of having seen him pass. While this feat required some extraordinary skills, obviously what one person can do is within the reach of others.

A very difficult way of being unseen is taught in various of the Oriental martial arts, and old reports suggest something similar was practiced by some American Indians. Essentially this method consists of quieting one's nervous and muscular systems to the point that no signals are transmitted to another person, so that the other person's perceptual apparatus is rendered ineffectual. According to this view, living organisms have to signal in some way their presence to other organisms in order to be perceived.

In the Old West, it was often remarked that some Indians could remain so still that people passing even within inches of them remained unaware of their existence. This is the way of being unseen that is most often taught in the martial arts, also in Yoga and in other spiritual disciplines. In Japan, martial artists called Ninja are famous for becoming virtually invisible.

There is one other method I have encountered, but I know of no instructions for achieving it. Twice, at dinner parties I have attended, where I found the conversation and the company especially boring, I was later told by those present that my chair had appeared empty throughout most of the dinner. I was unaware of this occurrence and would still like to know exactly how I managed it.

Chapter Three

Body Mysteries

To discover and catalog the unexplained abilities of the human body is to come to the conclusion that all of the studies devoted to the subject thus far have barely scratched the surface of what is to be known. And it seems as if the acquisition of one kind of knowledge about the human body casts much of the earlier knowledge into oblivion.

When one travels the world seeking out examples of bodily phenomena that should not be possible according to conventional Western allopathic medicine, it soon becomes evident that quite a number of lifetimes would be needed to adequately carry out the search. In many places in the world today, it is common to encounter "impossible" demonstrations of resistance to injury. One such example, fire-walking, has even come to the contemporary workshop circuit. And one can go further to find examples of men driving sharp-pointed daggers against their chests without piercing the flesh as the Balinese do, or running metal spikes through vital organs without pain, and with instant healing upon with-drawal of the object, as certain groups of Sufis can do.

In the case of Yoga, it has been demonstrated that control of virtually all "involuntary functions" can be achieved. This includes stopping the heart, altering the blood flow, self-regulating brain-wave activity, and much more. Around the world, there are to be discovered many effective healing practices that could not possibly work according to our understanding of the human body.

Most such extraordinary phenomena occur in the context of religion, spiritual disciplines and esoteric Schools. Often they work with souls, subtle bodies, "centers" and bodily energy systems, and with Gods and Goddesses, angels and demons, elemental spirits and spirits of the dead, and with many other forces.

I once came upon a school in Marrakech, Morocco, claiming continuous existence over many centuries which maintained that it worked with spirits whose special task it was to care for insane human beings. In this connection, they claimed that the spirits protected some of those who were mad by giving them access to various paranormal capacities.

It is an interesting fact, and has long been known, that mad-ness can liberate in a person powers like the *siddhis* of Yoga. For example, the generation of sufficient heat in one's body to keep it warm in even subfreezing temperatures is a *siddha*. A Yogi should be able to sit naked in a snow bank using his body heat to dry off one wet towel after another as it is draped over him. In the old asylums, it was often noted, and written about in medical journals, that even in subfreezing weather, some inmates would sleep naked on the stone floors without suffering either discomfort or damage.

Similarly, "hysterical" patients in mental hospitals were observed to handle live coals and to put their hands on hot stoves—again without discomfort or damage. This has been compared to the fire-walking done by some practitioners of martial arts.

Among the mad, the most accomplished "natural magicians" are the group of patients called schizophrenics. Schizophrenics are known to sometimes have extraordinarily strong immune systems and to exhibit abnormally rapid healing of wounds. In the so-called "fourth stage" of schizophrenia there may be little or no experience of pain. Such a patient might sit against a very hot radiator without any feeling of pain. In the reports I have seen, it is not mentioned whether the person was burned or not. (Of course, if the patient was reported not to have been burned, then the article probably would not be occurring in a contemporary scientific journal. Such journals today have much more fixed notions about what is possible than did their nineteenth and early twentieth-century predecessors. That which is regarded as "impossible" does not get published.)

Schizophrenics can be "energy vampires," draining anyone and everyone around them. They can also somehow manufacture a variety of stenches. I once had a patient, a very good-looking woman, who maintained, as some schizophrenics do, that her body had died. She was able, though not voluntarily or with conscious knowledge about how she did it, to make herself smell like a rotting corpse—a stink that somehow hovered just slightly this side of the intolerable.

I had an interesting experience with this woman. The fact that she was able to get in and out of a car and walk to my office, did not at all suffice to persuade her that her body was not dead. Neither could any other argument I could advance. I had been told that one psychiatrist had put ice cubes on her skin, held a candle flame close to her arm, and pricked her with a pin. She made no response and continued to insist that her body was dead. He was afraid of attempting any stronger stimulation.

I put her on a massage-type table and worked on one side of her body until it was different in almost every way from the other side. The side I worked on became substantially longer due to the lengthening of the muscles and the increased space in the joints, and lay flatter and lower than the other side. She was even breathing differently on the side I had worked on. On that side, if I picked up a leg or an arm, it was light as a feather, while the other side felt much, much heavier when I did the same thing. I kept this up for more than an hour and was pleased to note that she stopped smelling like a corpse.

Finally, the two sides were so differentiated that she could not deny that she felt a great difference between the two sides of her body. I helped her off the table, and when she walked, she became ever more aware of the difference between her two sides. She walked so much more quickly on one side that the other side had trouble keeping up. One arm moved much more freely than the other. One foot made much better contact with the floor. The breathing was much fuller on the side I had worked with and, when I showed her a mirror, she acknowledged that the eye on her "good side" was more vital looking than the other one.

As we talked about all this, she admitted for the first time that she could not be feeling what she was feeling if her body was dead.

Schizophrenics gain access to many other ordinarily latent capacities. They can be very telepathic and thus often become a threat to psychiatrists who have to deal with them. The mad, too, can be a valuable resource in exploring human potentials and some of the farther reaches of soma, soul and psyche.

I have tried to interest several psychiatrists who profess a strong interest in the paranormal and in human potentials to establish research projects to study the extraordinary phenomena some psychotic patients manifest. But psychiatrists in general are not interested in such phenomena as other than "pathological symptoms," and thus are unable to recognize the value of looking at the possible potentials of the "wild talents" they observe. One psychiatrist who, at my urging, proposed such a project not only was turned down by his hospital but his sanity was called into question!

Chapter Four

Body and
Inner Space Realities

While teaching in Stockholm some years ago, I was told a remarkable story by a Swedish psychiatrist who said he knew the case at firsthand. A man had been found dead in the freezer compartment of a train. The physician who examined him said that he exhibited every clinical symptom of having frozen to death. However, it was established that the compartment had been disconnected from any power source and the temperature inside could not have been any lower than forty-some degrees. But the man had evidently believed that the freezer unit was connected, and he must have slowly and painfully frozen to death in an Inner Space world of icy images. There was no other explanation available.

The psychiatrist put the emphasis on conscious belief, but it is less what the mind believes than what the brain accepts as its reality. The brain can be rather easily deceived by images, and images can take precedence over the material reality so that the images, not the material or objective reality, determine bodily responses—

even responses so complex as freezing to death. Moreover, as this case makes clear, the brain knows what to do apart from any past experience of the person. The dead man had doubtless been cold before, but he and his brain quite certainly had no past experience of freezing to death.

Changes in image bodies, such as a dream body for example, produce effects in the physical body. Boys learn this when they begin to have dreams about sex and the experience of the dream body causes the physical body to ejaculate—the so-called "wet dream." As a sexologist, I have studied such dreams and apparently a boy need not have had any previous sexual intercourse to experience, in the dream, sensations his physical body has never experienced. Memory is not required, something in the boy *already knows*, and that knowledge provides all that is required for the brain to bring about the sexual climax.

Sometimes, it would seem, past experience is required, sometimes not. Many physical responses to images experienced as virtual realities in trance can be demonstrated. If a hypnotic subject is told to hallucinate a burning candle and then to hold a finger over the flame, he or she will experience pain and then the finger will react as if to a real flame by forming a blister. If a person in trance is allergic to poison ivy and is handed an elm leaf while being told that the leaf is poison ivy, symptoms of ivy poisoning will develop. But if the person is handed an actual leaf of poison ivy and is told that it is an elm leaf, then no poisoning symptoms will develop. The leaf is perceived by the subject as being what it is said to be, and responses are to the perception and to the belief. But this experiment usually will not work unless the person has had some previous memory of ivy poisoning, so that there is an acquired knowledge of what the response will be.

Many examples can be given. For several days a person in trance who eats only hallucinated heavy meals will gain weight. Eventually some mechanism overrides that effect and hunger for objective food occurs. Within limits, suggestions about the weight of an object will determine the ease or difficulty with which it is lifted. Suggestions about odors will result in those odors being smelled, though no physical source of the odors is present. Apart from trance, many people with vivid sensory imaging capacities can achieve most of the same effects.

I was already impressed in my early teens by the fact that erotic dreams could produce orgasm and ejaculation. Pornographic and erotic writing, and photographs also, I learned, produced sexual responses in people, though not usually orgasm. The stimulation, like the responses, was simple and direct and involved strong appeal to emotions as well as enticing the mind to create images of personal involvement with what was being read about or looked at. The only literature and visual materials producing similar simple and direct responses in the body were the literature and visual images of horror. There was again a very strong appeal to emotions, the body became excited, and that excitement, though different, yielded a definite bodily pleasure. The brain was being played with, or played upon, by images. Such experiences could temporarily overwhelm and almost obliterate the ordinary reality where mind and images were much less dominant.

That the brain will respond to images it takes to constitute a reality opens up all sorts of possibilities. Medical hypnotists have sometimes successfully applied this knowledge to healing. For example, when the image of a tumor is sufficiently vivid, and it is suggested that the tumor is shrinking, then that effect may actually occur. The process can be continued until the tumor dwindles away completely. I know of quite a number of such cases, and my wife and I have worked together to twice remove a tumor from her breast when she had been told that surgery was absolutely required. The method assuredly does not work in all cases, and the reason why it does not work must be that the images were not real enough to the brain for the brain to do its work and eliminate the tumor.

Several years ago, I published a unique book, *Neurospeak*, containing some of the fruits of many years of exploration and thought concerning these matters. The book is unique because it is only necessary that a person read it as instructed to experience predictable and fairly complex changes in his or her body's sensing, movement capacities, musculoskcletal organization, and even brain wave production. There is no reliance on emotional or other strong stimulation to bring about these effects. The person does not do anything but read, avoiding voluntary movements or creation of images.

The text itself generates images in the unconscious that then act upon the brain and nervous system to generate involuntary micromovements in the muscles and other bodily effects. After reading a brief chapter about, say, the right shoulder, it will be found that that shoulder moves more freely than before and is sensed more clearly than before.

Only the part and functions read about will have changed. *Neurospeak* demonstrates, I believe, that almost any part or function of the body can be altered by means of the written or spoken word if only the effective language can be found to implant in the unconscious mind those images that will persuade the brain to bring about desired changes. Sometimes one deceives the brain as to what is actually taking place. In other instances it is only necessary to provide it with effective directions.

The Inner Space traveler should know that the physical body is responsive to experiences of realities that seem far removed from the everyday world and the reality consensus. This fact affords both opportunities and risks, and such examples as those I have just mentioned will be instructive and useful if given some careful thought and then applied to the journeying.

Chapter Five

Living Goddess
of Kathmandu

About in the center of Kathmandu, capital of Nepal, there is a palatial building with a very large ground floor room. At one end of that huge room, well up above the ground floor, there is a balcony. On a throne at the center of that balcony, there sits a young girl, elaborately costumed and with her face heavily painted. She is the Living Goddess.

The girl sits on the throne for many hours each day while large numbers of people come into the big room to see her and be in her presence. I have observed more than one of these Living Goddesses over the years and they appear to be remarkably similar in almost every way. This is especially true of the lack of movement in the body, including even the eyes. She seems to be in a trance, rarely blinks, and never seems to pay any attention to the people coming and going in the room. She seems to occupy her space as an idol does, indwelled by some force and available to be experienced and worshipped, but without any apparent awareness of others.

This Living Goddess is, however, far from immortal or even very long-lasting. The official astrologers, using ancient time-honored and exceedingly refined calculations, determine just when and where the Living Goddess is to be found. She is identified and located at about the same time that the Living Goddess she will succeed is ready to menstruate for the first time. When this menstruation occurs, the Living Goddess becomes no longer acceptable and is replaced.

The Living Goddess begins her "tenure" at about the age of six and remains in her role until, as mentioned, she menstruates, and another Living Goddess takes her place. During the time she is Living Goddess, this girl will be a virtual prisoner, although a well-treated one according to the standards of that tradition.

Once she is no longer Living Goddess, however, the girl's life abruptly changes. She is returned to her parents, usually in some small village, and will become a kind of pariah and so remain throughout her life. No one will marry her. No one will give her work. She probably will never have friends—she is, after all, not a human being.

The former Living Goddess will remain with her parents for as long as they can take care of her and, after that, will live with her brothers or sisters, or some other relatives, whose obligation it will be to support her. It is a very difficult situation for everyone concerned.

Much of the life of the Living Goddess is kept secret. What does she do when she is not sitting on her throne? It is impossible to find out what she is taught, if she ever plays, or what, in other ways, her life is like. Above all, one must wonder what does she think and what does she feel? With her heavily painted face never changing its expression, and her elaborately costumed immobile body, the Living Goddess sitting there on her throne seems completely inscrutable. She is so impassive as to give the impression of being in some extraordinary kind of deep trance. It could be that she has been taught to meditate, but more likely she is in a state of possession by whatever system of energies she, for a few years, embodies during the time she serves.

Since one Living Goddess looks just like another, it strengthens the impression that there is some constellation of energies, a "Something" paranormal and possibly nonhuman, that endures, possessing, animating and otherwise making use of the endless succession of young girls who sit on the Kathmandu throne as Living Goddess from one generation to the next, one century to the next, possibly to continue for as long as Nepal itself endures.

I have often wondered if being a Goddess for a few years could be rewarding enough to compensate for all the sacrifices these girls have to make.

Chapter Six

A Thought Form

There was a fine French artist, Jean Despujols, who was living in Shreveport, Louisiana, when I knew him. He had accomplished hundreds of paintings of Angkor Vat, the great Cambodian temple complex, some of them visionary works portraying beautiful bodies of dancers glowing from within and radiating a preternatural light. When I went to see him, he told me about an experiment he once participated in, a group effort to create a thought form, or image made material and animated so as to possess the appearance, and some characteristics, of a living being. (I will discuss thought forms further in my next tale, and those who wish to pursue the matter in more detail might consult the classic work by Alexandra David-Neel, *Magic and Mystery in Tibet*.)

As I recall it, the other participants, all men of eminence, included a physician, a judge, a diplomat and another gentleman or two, along with Despujols. All shared an interest in psychic phenomena and they agreed to meet once each week and attempt, by means of their collective concerted concentration, to create a thought form. They had been mainly inspired by the Tibetan tradition as described by Madame David-Neel and others having firsthand as well as scholarly knowledge of Tibetan Buddhist and other magical and occult sources.

The men would meet in a room rented for the experiment and not used at any other time. There were several locks on the door, to which no one had more than one key. After entering the room the men would seal the door with wax and tape, so that it could not be opened undetected. The room's window would be similarly sealed.

Then they would sit down, achieve deep relaxation, and each would try to project into the same space the image of a tiger. They met many times, until finally the conviction was shared that, in the place concentrated on, there could be perceived what looked like particles of energy, as if something was becoming material.

The effort continued, week after week, the thought form seeming to become stronger, clearer, definitely recognizable as possessing three-dimensional being. One, then another, and another, began to perceive the general size and shape of a tiger. There was a mounting expectancy and, also, although not yet admitted, an increasing anxiety. Then, as Despujols recounted, there occurred the final meeting of the group.

Concerning this meeting, he spoke only for himself—but, finally, the tiger appeared. It was not just a real tiger, but surreal, archetypal. Evidently, in that instant, most of all those present perceived it. The tiger was ferocious, menacing, and it began to advance, snarling, upon its creators.

A Thought Form

Then, suddenly, there was an explosion in the room. Later, it was speculated, the anxiety caused everyone to simultaneously break off concentration. The tiger was gone, but the window was shattered. The broken glass was not inside the room, but outside, so that the explosion was within the room. A thorough search was made and revealed no objective reason why the blast should have occurred. Inquiries disclosed nothing outside the room that might suggest any physical cause for the phenomenon.

By mutual consent of all, the experiment ended. Any speculation that the group had created nothing more than a "collective hallucination" seemed to be conclusively refuted.

Chapter Seven

Living Images

The creation of the thought form is an effort pursued most exhaustively in Tibet where it is said to have reached its highest level of accomplishment in modern times. Western observers as well as the Tibetans have repeatedly described the creation by mental means of *tulpas*, or thought forms, usually in the form of human beings and animals. These have the appearance of being completely natural but are said to be able to exist for only brief periods of time—hours, days, perhaps weeks. However, there have been occasional reports of *tulpas* created in their own likeness by very high lamas—*tulpas* enduring for months, or even years, in order to bring to completion work with pupils who would otherwise never receive the finished knowledge from their deceased Teachers.

A very arduous and prolonged training in vivification and concentrated holding of visual images is said to be required before the thought form can be produced. The individual, in order to be able to produce a *tulpa*, works for years to strengthen his visual imagery. He first learns to produce and sustain very vivid images with his eyes closed. After that, he learns to externalize or hallucinate his images, projecting them outward into the external world. If he is an artist, he learns to project the image of what he will paint onto the surface to be painted and then he simply goes over the projected image with his tools and his paints. When he is at this level of development, his externalized images are visible only to himself and perhaps to his Teachers. Finally the imagery capacity becomes so powerful that the externalized image is substantial enough to be perceived by anyone. More work with other sensory images enables the *tulpa* to move and to touch, see, hear, and so on.

More extraordinary still, it is held that certain images can be infused with mental energies that give them a kind of autonomy, or volition of their own, for the duration of their existence. It is said that a few of the more durable *tulpas*, because of this autonomy, occasionally escape and live lives of their own. Moreover, they are material enough to convincingly interact with ordinary human beings. They develop more or less as individuals, possessing rather simple minds and a spectrum of feelings. They speak the language of their creator, can move material objects, and they can become violent, inflicting injury. Evidently their mental stability is precarious, since there is no physical brain and nervous system to allow for adequate adaptation to new circumstances outside the inherited memories and capacities of their creator.

It is but rarely intended, however, that a *tulpa*, whether in human or animal form, should go very far from the place of its creation and the person who created it. The *tulpa* is almost always intended to function as a servant, attending to various needs and desires of its human creator. In ancient times, history or legend has it, magicians in other parts of the world also had thought forms as assistants, but the prolonged and intense concentration needed to bring such an entity into existence is said to be too demanding for Westerners living among all of the distractions of contemporary societies.

I have read and often have been told about these matters but have not personally met anyone who claims to have had definitive firsthand acquaintance with a *tulpa*. However, they remain a persistent presence in the magical and occult lore, and the notion that images can have a material reality will certainly one day, I believe, be supported by incontrovertible scientific evidence. At present such evidence remains anecdotal, but voluminous. If the account provided by Despujols, in my previous tale, is authentic—and I believe it to be so—then experimentation, done so as to silence reasonable dispute, will provide such evidence. Physics will eventually render a plausible explanation.

Chapter Eight

Psychedelic Experience

LSD-25, and plants such as the peyote cactus with its mescaline alkaloids, or psilocybe mushrooms, open wide the portals of Inner Space and can provide a diversity and richness of experiences not accessible by any other means. Virtually every Inner Space experience possible to body, mind or spirit can become accessible to the traveler when psychedelic plants or drugs provide entry and when the traveler's life has equipped him or her for what will be experienced. Just as with experiences in the world of normal reality, what happens to the person will always depend to some extent on who and what that person is.

In the late 1940s I lived for some months in Paris and spent many nights in West Bank cafes listening to Jean-Paul Sartre, Simone de Beauvoir, and other French intellectuals and philosophers talk about existentialist philosophy. Some American authors I esteemed were also part of those gatherings from time to time—John Steinbeck, Erskine Caldwell and Richard Wright among them.

I was fascinated, as were many in those years, by the existentialist blending of philosophy and psychoanalysis, by Sartre especially. I was too inexperienced to recognize how profoundly paranoid that philosophy was, but I might have recognized it had I given thought to Sartre's experience with mescaline, and known enough to relate it to his philosophy. The drug, which would open up a heaven to many, opened up for Sartre only hell. Objects he looked at and touched turned into skulls and corpses with rotting flesh, and other horrors. For at least a year after that "trip," Sartre hallucinated terrifying images. Giant crayfish would follow him down the street, and the doors of houses turned into mouths with teeth that gnashed and threatened to devour him. The dread of objectification by the Other—the Other as the vampire that sucks away one's freedom—was clearly deep-rooted in Sartre's unconscious, and entered into his conscious experience and also into existentialist philosophy. The philosophy somehow struck a chord in the post-World War II psyche, and many people, intellectuals especially, were influenced and damaged by it. Sartre's brilliance seduced them. His mescaline experience showed what resided at the core of his being.

Another major intellectual figure of the time, Aldous Huxley, had an altogether different kind of experience with mescaline. If Sartre's experience was of Hell, Huxley's was of Heaven. He described it in two books, *The Doors of Perception* and *Heaven and Hell*, the first book published in 1954. It may be said to have ushered in the psychedelic era and movement of the '60s and '70s.

By contrast to Sartre, Huxley described experiences of fantastic worlds resembling the paradises of myths and scriptures. There were vast expanses of gems and semiprecious stones across which moved legendary beasts such as unicorns and dragons, and human and superhuman figures of extraordinary beauty. There were a variety of worlds without end, and they were such that no artist could have painted or sculpted them. There were colors such as Huxley had never seen before, and a preternatural light unlike anything found in the everyday world, but suggested—no words could possibly describe them—by the literatures of visionary and mystical experience.

Huxley was struck by the fact that these could not possibly be creations of his own mind, and they were certainly not memories. This, he believed, was a real world of real beings. The images were not like the archetypes of Jung, they had no meaning apart from themselves, and they were symbolic of nothing belonging either to the personal or collective unconscious. His experience was one of "the veil was lifted that I might see." These worlds were always there and our everyday world as we knew it was only a "measly trickle" of the larger reality we might know if our blinders were removed. The effects of mescaline continue for as long as twelve hours, and what is seen, and otherwise sensed, sometimes seems to exceed what occurs during years of clock-measured time and normal consciousness. Huxley went on to describe a great many more wondrous experiences made accessible to him by mescaline, and concluded that they are of inestimable value. Psychology, philosophy, and many other fields of knowledge are woefully incomplete without the knowledge psychedelic exploration makes possible.

After reading Huxley's book, in 1954, I immediately found a way to begin my own explorations with the peyote cactus and its mescaline alkaloids. I had only to write off to a nursery in Laredo, Texas, to promptly have sent to me crates of fine-looking, and very potent, peyote buttons. I would continue such explorations for decades, and would assuredly have made them my life's work had laws not been passed making use of psychedelics illegal. In New York, my wife-to-be, Jean Houston, was part of a medical research team working with LSD-25. I joined her in that work and eventually, in addition to my own exploring, we were able to report on the experiences of more than two hundred research subjects.

After we were married, Jean and I wrote a book, *The Varieties of Psychedelic Experience*, reporting on what we had learned. Psychedelic experiences of artists launched an art movement and we wrote an account of that in another book, *Psychedelic Art*. There are in fact so many varieties of the psychedelic experience that probably no amount of writing could ever exhaust the subject.

My first experience was in some respects much like Huxley's. Whether my eyes were closed or open, there was incredible beauty. With the eyes closed, there were the vast seas of gems, and the mythic and legendary creatures he had seen. With my eyes open, everything became a wondrous work of art. At one point I heard an orchestra of what must have been hundreds of instruments playing—music that simply went beyond anything I had ever heard, and seemed to include sounds made by instruments which, to my knowledge, do not exist on this earth. And I do not even play an instrument! Marveling at this, I played a recording of Bach, my favorite composer. It was an immensely complex composition, but as I listened to it I found it so simple and crude as to offend my intelligence. I could not understand that experience unless I concluded that there had been such an alteration of my brain's capacities as to make me, for the moment, vastly more intelligent with respect to music than I had ever been. I disliked that experience and went on to look at some favorite works of art. But those, for the moment, were reduced to clumsy cartoons.

I then found myself out of my body, a consciousness floating up near the ceiling. I had never really believed in out-of-body experiences, but that one seemed quite real. During that experience I had observed that there were some papers on the floor behind my sofa that could not be seen while standing on the floor. By climbing a ladder I was able to see them exactly as I'd previously observed them while out of my body.

Thousands of other phenomena occurred on that day. I had spent much time studying philosophy and psychoanalysis, but it seemed to me I learned more in twelve hours of my mescaline experience than in years at the university and in private studies. I devoted myself to philosophical thinking and found that my concentration was unwavering and exceeded anything of which I had ever been capable before. I thought about Sartre, and existentialism, and ideas that had been damaging to me. I spent more than an hour doing that and discovered that I was thinking my way free of those ideas. After that day, I would have one mescaline experience almost every week for two years, and I would devote two hours of each twelve-hour experience to examining philosophical ideas long of special interest to me. During the week preceding I would refresh myself with respect to those ideas, and I always found that the mescaline, by enabling me to concentrate so completely, provided new ideas and insights important for my self-understanding and freedom. I thoroughly exorcised Sartre and existentialism from my mind and emotions during that period.

This aspect of Inner Space experience—the possibility of prolonged and concentrated thinking—has received almost no attention. It did underlie, though rarely recognized by the people, some feats of creative problem solving achieved by a few of our research subjects.

LSD-25 provided me, as it did others, with powerful religious experiences we felt met all the criteria for the authenticity of such experiences as established by the recognized authorities. In my case, there appeared to me, in my room, what I knew to be the Kundalini serpent, a manifestation of the Egyptian Goddess Sekhmet, about seven or eight feet in height, composed of flowing energies and colors, and somehow reaching out to draw me into its presence. This experience was, and is, unique in my entire life. The manifestation was, in fact, Wholly Other, and filled me with such awe at its beauty, and rapture at my sensing of its energies, that feelings of love and adoration overwhelmed me—awe and rapture never felt by me before or since. Then I knew, with absolute certainty, that this was more real than any reality known to me, and that never again would I be able to doubt the existence of the divine and the numinous. Every experience of my life paled by comparison to this one. All my other experiences, including religious and mystical ones, I now understood, were of only partial realities. This one was fundamental and absolute. I don't know how long the revelation and the rapture lasted, but it was long enough for me to know that I had been granted a certitude never to be shaken or challenged by any doubts.

Countless other strange and powerful experiences occurred during the psychedelic explorations. I will mention just one more. With a friend, I sat before a curious drawing done by one of the psychedelic artists, Allan Atwell. It is a large drawing of a man, life-sized, seated in a Yoga posture, with the interior of his body, including chakras or centers, visible (Plate 1). This drawing was done, Atwell told me, according to an ancient Tibetan formula he had learned while living in India, and if the drawing is meditated on successfully, then, first, human bodies will become transparent; after that, if a second phase of the meditation is successful, the meditator will receive a vision of the Void.

We focused intently on the drawing—for how long, I have no idea. But our bodies did eventually become transparent to one another. We stood facing each other, lost in the wonder of the experience, when I saw a yellowish object in my friend's womb. I told her what I saw and she said, yes, there was a tumor and she was to have surgery the next day. She had not mentioned it because she feared that might spoil our experience.

Her body seemed very subtle and insubstantial and I told her I thought I could reach into her body and extract the tumor. She asked me to do it, and I reached through her belly and, in fact, removed it, or that was our shared perception. It was about the size of a golf ball and yellowish in color. I held it in the palm of my hand and, as we watched, it began to shrink, until it dwindled away altogether, and nothing was left of it.

The next day she called me to say that it had been determined that the tumor no longer existed and she would not have the surgery. It did not surprise me that an image of a tumor shrinking and disappearing can actually shrink, and even eliminate, a tumor. If the brain accepts the reality of the event, then it can execute what is imaged. That has happened a number of times in my experience, and in the literature of hypnosis there are many such cases. But the transparency of our bodies was unique, although in Yoga and some other spiritual disciplines there are statements about that possibility.

The friend with whom I shared this experience was with me on a number of Inner Space excursions. She would always have a wonderful time but often, at the very end of the experience, she would panic. The earth would fall away just behind her, and that experience then would be transmitted to me. We would then run through the woods out behind my house as if pursued by the hounds of Hell, with the Abyss nipping at our heels. Then, all at once, the LSD effects would wear off and the experience would be over, with the earth solid all around us. There are endless varieties of the psychedelic experience.

One day our society will come to understand that psychedelic drugs provide the best access yet to the contents and processes of the human mind. Then, as so many of us who have had experiences with psychedelics have urged, explorations of Inner Space will be regarded as being at least equally as important as those of Outer Space. However, Inner Space exploration must include many diffcrent kinds of explorers, and it must be kept free.

Chapter Nine

Concerning Messengers and Guides

It is likely that at least some readers will be motivated to undertake travels and explorations to get to know for themselves firsthand what they are reading about. Since I have spent a good part of more than half a century being personally involved in such explorations and travels, I will provide throughout this book quite a few "travel tips" and other hopefully helpful pieces of information. I consider that the information in this tale and the next one is likely to be of particular value.

In imaginal worlds there are many messengers. Often they are animals, hybrid combinations of animals, and other figures part-animal, part-human in form. There are many serpents, and lions with and without wings. Figures with human bodies and the heads and wings of birds appear to Inner Space voyagers at many levels of consciousness and reside in or do the work of what seem to be numerous and quite different worlds.

These guides and messengers have been depicted in art since the most ancient times and throughout most of history. Sometimes the Gods have superficially similar forms, but it is not likely that anyone will mistake a god for a messenger. However, it should be mentioned that someone who has never been in the presence of deity might mistake a messenger for a god or goddess. But the messenger does not pretend to such status and will set right the confusion. It may be that an evil demon on occasion creates an illusion to assume the appearance of deity in order to entrap or seduce a mortal. But the punishment for such a deception is said to be severe enough to make the act a rare one.

If a messenger comes from a god or a goddess, some evidence of this is usually offered—an emblem or seal—or it may be that a likeness of the god or goddess is a part of the messenger's body. For example, the identifying mark may be in the palm of the hand, or on the bottom of a paw or foot. Or the sign may be somewhere else. False credentials of this kind may be presented, but again the crime is considered heinous and its punishment severe.

The messenger or guide either leads or transports a person all or part of the way to the person's destination. One might, for instance, descend into watery depths on the back of a serpent, or be borne through the air on the back of some gigantic winged creature. In general, messengers and guides inspire confidence and trust: they do not engender fear. If a traveler feels fear, then beware, there is some serious fault. This fault may be in the messenger or guide, but it also may be in the traveler, who for some reason is impure or unworthy. At this point a traveler can, and should, turn back.

In addition to messengers and guides of the aforementioned

types, there are ones who take many other forms: some appear to be lights, small globes of fire, or suns. Sometimes a traveler is scooped up by a whirlwind or borne by the currents of a river or a sea. Of course, there are also those cases where no messenger or guide appears at all; the traveler is just all at once transported to his or her destination. If a messenger or guide does appear, it may be a Teacher, so that some essential preliminary knowledge is imparted along the way to the destination. In other cases, it may be that the guide's role is to help the traveler make a gradual approach toward the destination, allowing the traveler time to adjust and make a good transition into the different reality. And there are other reasons, too many to enumerate, why the guide or messenger may be needed.

The confidence inspired by these figures enables those travelers who might not otherwise be able to do so to move without difficulty through environments of water and fire and vast empty reaches of space where breathing would be impossible if there were fear or doubt. Evil spirits, ferocious monsters and other adversaries may be encountered along the way, and the messenger or guide gives protection against such kinds of forces, which might otherwise destroy the person by causing death or madness.

Those travelers, especially inexperienced ones, but in some cases veteran explorers as well, who imprudently wander alone through imaginal worlds may be in danger. Not only are there fiends and monsters and demons, there are psychic carnivores and spirits seeking to possess a human being. A wise external guide, another person, knowledgeable of imaginal worlds, can offer protection against most of these destructive entities. But a guide belonging to those worlds and having all the authority of some potent deity is the best protection—excepting, always, an actual Being of Power, god or goddess, or some other being of high rank in the hierarchy of Forces.

Chapter Ten

The Turtle

It has been my experience over many decades, both as a magician and as an explorer, that the turtle encountered in Inner Space is almost invariably a friendly or benign figure, indicating progress and furthering progression towards a worthwhile goal.

Very small turtles are rare in Inner Space; turtles larger than those to be found in the ordinary reality are the rule.

The turtle frequently appears as a means of transport, that is as a large turtle a traveler can ride. Not rarely, a comfortable chair or stool is affixed to the giant turtle's back. One seats oneself on the back of the turtle and the turtle may seem to move slowly. Nonetheless, this is a comparatively rapid means of getting to a destination already established, but of which the conscious mind does not have any knowledge.

The turtle is also a good means of descent to more profoundly altered states of consciousness; mounting the turtle, or simply clinging to the turtle, one descends through watery depths. The weight of the turtle encourages a swift descent, and the turtle has the capacity to become heavier and more dense, to increase its capacity to descend deeper and more swiftly, but the turtle does not spontaneously exercise this capacity. The transformation is elicited by an interaction between the human being and the turtle, the person providing instructions about what is wanted.

The turtle can be a protector—the need for protection arises rather seldom when the Inner Space traveler is with the turtle, whose potency is better understood by destructive forces than by the person involved with this particular image or symbol system. The jaws of the turtle are very powerful, the shell especially protective, and the turtle can bring the person under cover of the shell.

The turtle is responsive to affection, whether provided verbally, by touch, or otherwise expressed. For example, the turtle especially likes to be fed; it is omnivorous. The spirit in which a gift is given is of much greater importance to the turtle than what is given.

The eye of the Inner Space turtle is sharp, resembling that of the eagle or the hawk in appearance. However, the impression of farsightedness is an illusion. In fact, it is a frailty of the turtle that its vision is limited. Because of this basic frailty, the turtle is a short-range guide, usually performing a kind of shuttle service between guides able to offer more long-range capacities. For example, a lion may meet the traveler at the place to which the turtle has brought him or her, the turtle having met the traveler at a place where he or she had been brought and set down by a birdman.

The turtle may have a protective magic circle on its back, in cases where this is needed. The traveler who is met by such a turtle will know that she or he is under attack, but protected by powerful forces. If there are candles burning around the circle on the back of the turtle, both the protection and the attacker should be understood as unusually potent.

Because of the importance of the archetypal turtle, injury to turtles (and tortoises) must be avoided; if a turtle or tortoise is injured in the ordinary reality, the functioning of the Inner Space turtle may be impaired. An Inner Space turtle with a burning candle on its back bears light. It is sometimes recommended to place a candle on the back of an ordinary turtle or tortoise if you wish to be guided in Inner Space by a symbolic one. In magic, that is, or at least used to be, a well-known practice.

Chapter Eleven

A Revival of Gargoyles

Many entities are rising again in our time that were supposed to have been banished forever into other dimensions or were believed to belong to the fantasy worlds of our superstitious forebears. Gargoyles are among these.

Strictly speaking, the word gargoyle—*garguille* in its original French—is nothing more than a water spout. Such figures evidently first appeared on French Gothic cathedrals and were made in a number of deliberately grotesque forms intended to frighten evil spirits away from the House of God. The most famous gargoyles are those to be found high on the cathedral of Notre Dame de Paris (Plate 2). But many other gargoyles adorn churches and other buildings wherever this particular Roman Catholic art has made its way into architecture.

It is unclear whether the sculptures were made in the likeness of legendary beings whose appearances were known, or were imaginary creations of the cathedral sculptors. The gargoyles often resemble demons and monsters from a much more remote past.

After the creation of the sculptured gargoyles, however, there came to be a lore of gargoyles as actual beings. This lore continues up to the present time, and in recent years various persons have reported making contact with gargoyles. In fact, a group of magicians has arisen that claims to have received a fairly elaborate system of "gargoyle magic." There has even been published one Grimoire, or operating manual, of such magic, with others said to be forthcoming.

One of the most interesting observations about gargoyles was made by P. D. Ouspensky, recalling an observation made by his Teacher, the very saintly Mr. Gurdjieff. Gurdjieff pointed out that the gargoyles on the Notre Dame Cathedral in Paris had a very singular quality. If a person was photographed standing next to one of the gargoyles, then the gargoyle would seem to be much more alive than the human—or the human would seem to be more like the sculpture.

I have had the very unusual experience of watching what seemed to be a gargoyle take possession of a human body. Gargoyles are said to be about the size of elves, somewhere around four feet in height, very bony, with the upper body slanting triangularly down to a very thin waist, and the face also being quite triangular with the bones clearly showing.

On more than one occasion, I, and some of my students, observed a female magician who appeared possessed by a gargoyle in such a way that the whole structure of her body and face changed. These took on the characteristic triangular appearance, and her bones strained against her flesh and her skin was stretched so tautly that it seemed her body might explode. Her body also appeared to be about one foot shorter than it had been. This "being" called herself simply Garguille, and she was very shy and frightened in human company. Her behavior was what one might expect of a wild creature suddenly finding itself in a room full of people.

This Garguille was able, with difficulty, to use the brain and vocal chords of the body she was possessing, and so was able to speak. She said that it was too painful for her to remain very long in that body, and too dangerous for the human, and so she would have to go. She said she would try to return on some future occasions.

She did, in fact, return twice more, but never could stay very long. The woman whose body she possessed was so terribly contorted and strained that it really did seem too dangerous to continue to explore these experiences. To this day, that manifestation of Garguille remains one of the most unusual examples of possession that I have ever seen.

Chapter Twelve

Points of No Return

In the worlds of religious, mystical, magical and occult practices and spiritual disciplines, it is possible to find examples—happily rare—of Inner Space explorers who lose their way. Most of such casualties are those who may be said to have gone so far in that they cannot find their way back. Much more rare are those who have gone so far out that they, too, cannot return.

The usual example of the latter is the person who has thoroughly developed the capacity for "out-of-body experiences." The out-of-body experience is a quite real one—the consciousness goes out of the physical body and travels to more or less distant places, but almost always in the external world. That is to say, the out-of-body traveler may frequently go to Kansas, but rarely, if ever, goes to an Inner Space mythical world such as Oz. In various occult and magical traditions, cases of people who have gone so far out they cannot find their way back are described. The body continues to live, but it is as if the mind has departed.

Only the most rudimentary bodily functions then are possible. The body can be fed, and it may be led about and even eventually be trained to obey a few commands, about as a normally intelligent dog is able to do. Beings of this kind may be created, it is said, by means of certain black magical practices that entice the mind and soul out of the body, and then ensnare them, preventing them from returning to the body. One thinks of the zombies of Haiti and of some similar creatures known in Africa and Asia.

Less rare are examples of individuals—deliberate explorers and accidental voyagers—who go so far in that they then cannot find their way out. Such persons actually go beyond the limits, reaching a literal point of no return, and of course are not heard from again. We know about them, or think that we do, rather as we know about an explorer who is last seen entering some dark and dangerous region where cannibals and headhunters live—and, after that, is never seen again.

In myths and legends there are similar stories—at the other extreme—of explorers who are last seen at the portals of some kind of paradise, who never return and are therefore presumed to have found an existence so pleasurable or otherwise rewarding that they elected not to come back. The story of Shangri-la is an example, and there are innumerable reports from people who have come close to death and who have been tempted to pass permanently over into the paradises they perceived. Many who do come back after having penetrated very far into Inner Space describe entering regions where the body and mind experience such ecstasy, rapture and bliss that the desire not to come back is little short of overwhelming. Like a diver experiencing the rapture of the deep, one profoundly craves to keep going deeper even while knowing that at some point it will be impossible to return.

I should add that there are considerably more frequent instances of persons who go very far in, and who seem to be irretrievable, but who will eventually return if one simply waits them out. I have seen this occur with persons in very deep trance states following unusually prolonged induction and deepening procedures. Such a person becomes unresponsive to words and to any other sensory stimulation and may remain in that condition for hours. In most cases the trance will eventually pass over into sleep and the person will eventually awaken to his or her ordinary state of consciousness.

Inexperienced people working with or observing such trances sometimes panic when the hypnotized person will not come out of trance. The inexperienced person may behave in stupid and irrational ways and inflict psychological or even physical trauma on the one who is in trance as they resort to extreme measures to bring the person back. Violently shaking the person in trance, or pounding on the person, is not all that unusual and can do physical harm as well as being terrifying to someone who comes out of a profound trance under those circumstances. The person in trance may be very empathic as well and become infected in the trance reality by the panic of the one who is trying to bring that person out of the profoundly altered state. The result can be a chronic anxiety neurosis, or even madness.

I used to be hopeful that in cases of these extraordinarily deep trances the person—when finally emerging from the trance—could shed some light on what happens to those rare people who go in and then never do come out. The person emerging from such a long, profound trance is always amnesiac. However, I hoped that if they went back into trance they would be able to regain some memory of what had happened on the previous occasion. I was never successful in this. It was as if there exists some portal or boundary beyond which experiences occur that are not accessible to the conscious mind. As people recross that boundary, on the way back to realms of experience where memories are retrievable, they no longer possess the capacity to recall the other side.

There are myths and legends about wonderful worlds or places protected by these boundaries. The person who has experienced one of those Paradises loses all memory once she or he passes beyond its borders. In this way the Paradise is protected from being overwhelmed by the multitude of people who would go there if they knew of its existence.

There are people who specialize in retrieving and bringing effectively back into their physical bodies persons who have lost their way by going too far in or too far out. Such experiences were evidently more common in times when more people went very seriously and very rigorously searching for God and for the spiritual dimensions of Being. The ones who specialized in finding those who are lost were called Fishers of Souls. Today the problems of such lost psyches and souls will almost always be handed over to psychiatrists, who are not equipped to understand what has happened, or that such things are possible. Even less are those medical specialists trained for the task of an effective retrieval.

Chapter Thirteen

A Regression Experiment

As is well known, it is possible to use "hypnotic regression" to enable a person to apparently revivify experiences the person has had earlier.

For example, one can suggest to a forty-year-old woman that she is going back in time to her twentieth birthday, or her fifteenth, or her tenth. If the regression is successful, she will experience herself as she was at that time. She may also find herself in the place where she was when at the exact age being suggested to her, in some cases down even to a precise date and time. The ability of a person to regress in this way is not only fascinating, but can be used to explore old traumas and also bring about healings, physical as well as psychological ones.

It is also the case that many of the "memories" retrieved by means of hypnotic regression are only fantasies, while some may be suggested to the subject or patient by the therapist or other hypnotist. In recent years, therapists with certain axes to grind have countless times dredged up "memories" of sexual molestations that were definitely false and that led to great harm being done to the person doing the "remembering" as well as to those accused and others who might have then become involved. Other false memories, too, can do major damage, and great caution and high levels of competence are needed when such regression and attempted recovery of important experiences are involved.

It is questionable just how far back in life a person can be regressed. Some researchers and therapists claim to get authentic experiences of very early childhood and even of birth or of life in the womb.

Some people, who believe in reincarnation, also believe that it is possible in a hypnotic trance to gain recollection of a past life or lives. Some people, who have been regressed repeatedly into one of these "past lives" have had such rich experiences as to enable them to write books about it. The best-selling book *The Search for Bridie Murphy* touched off a host of them. Most hypnotists who consider that they are taking a scientific approach deny that these regressions to past lives are possible. Noting that hypnosis makes possible very rich sensory and other images, so that the trance world constitutes a "virtual reality," they concede that the person claiming the experience of a past life may believe that what they have described is real.

I have done regressions with hundreds of people and have witnessed quite a number of others. Most of these "regressions" I regard as fantasies, and yet there remains a mysterious residue of experiences that I can neither reject nor authenticate. A psychiatrist once devised an experiment that he hoped would test the authenticity of hypnotic regression. It was extremely ingenious since he decided that he would attempt a phylogenetic regression, not just back through "past lives" but even to a prehuman state of being.

He did an experiment in which a woman was regressed many times along her own life span and then back through any possible past lives to a prehuman existence. From that point on, she began to manifest behavior characteristic of a chimpanzee—behavior with which the psychiatrist was familiar. The hypnotic subject was semi-literate and presumably had no prior knowledge of subprimate behavior. Nonetheless, no matter what the test, she made correct chimpanzee responses.

One of those responses was extremely dramatic. For reasons unknown, a chimpanzee is one of several creatures that experience horror at the sight of a severed head. The woman was shown the head of a clothing store mannequin and she then evidenced such panic that the experimenters feared for her life. As had been worked out in advance for these sessions, she was brought back by means of prearranged signals, since she could no longer understand human speech.

However they are to be explained, there are examples from any number of times and places of the apparent transformation of human beings into animals—ones that do not seem to be cases of either self-delusion or, from those outside, hallucination. The footsteps of the human become the tracks of the beast as the matter moves into the more profound dimensions of mystery. At the same time, the experiment just mentioned points, as does other evidence, to altered states of consciousness, spontaneous or induced, as the most likely explanation and the most indicated path of exploration.

Chapter Fourteen

Far Out Healings

When in India, I was told of swamis of Yoga, Tantric magicians, and other holy men, living in caves in the Himalayas, who described themselves as having maintained themselves in deep trances, or other altered states of consciousness, for many months and even years. Some of these Inner Space dwellers never returned to the ordinary reality at all, though they could communicate with their disciples as a person in a drug or trance state communicates with other people. At the same time, they were at some sort of midpoint, where they could communicate with equal ease with entities and even sometimes deities in other, still farther out reality dimensions. The Inner Space dwellers passed along to their disciples the fruits of their dialogues with higher entities. The Teacher's body remained in the world of the disciples, ate and slept and excreted there, but the body was all that remained there.

It was said that the bodies were typically in excellent health, aged very slowly, and died at advanced ages, of one hundred years or even considerably more. Those health and longevity factors were attributed to the mind's inhabiting Inner Space.

As I pondered these tales, I remembered the famous case in Paris of the so-called Sleeping Beauty of the *Hotel Dieu*. A beautiful young woman was brought to that hospital in a coma from which she never emerged. She remained there in the coma for half a century until she died. During all that time she retained her beauty and her youth, and physicians, philosophers and others from many countries came to see the world-famous Sleeping Beauty. No one could adequately explain why her body appeared not to age. Can it be, I wondered, that if one is removed far enough from the so-called reality consensus, then one also gets beyond the reach of time and the effects of time on the human body? Probably everyone who has experienced LSD or some other potent psychedelic knows that there can be a vast difference between the amounts of experience possible in Inner Space, on the one hand, and the everyday world of clock-measured time, on the other. I used to wonder if having so much more experience within units of clock-measured time would result in premature aging of the human body. That does not seem to happen. But may it be possible to enter into realms so far from our own that there is comparatively no time in those realms, and thus no aging, or aging taking place so slowly as to be unnoticeable? Did the Sleeping Beauty of the *Hotel Dieu* die of old age despite her seeming youth, or did she die of something else? No cause of death was evident. Her case always seemed to me to demonstrate that the aging process need not be at all like what we now observe it to be—at least not when the mind is dwelling where it appears that other laws govern.

Also, when I heard these accounts of Inner Space dwellers, I was reminded of the work of a healer I had learned about some years earlier. In the late nineteenth century, in Stockholm, Sweden, a physician named Otto Wetterstrand experimented with the theory that what he called "prolonged sleep"—actually prolonged somnambulistic, or very deep, trance—was a powerful therapeutic force. He described the successful treatment of a wide array of physical and nervous disorders, including epilepsy, hysteria, insomnia, severe prolonged headaches and other pain, problems of digestion, menstruation and many other disorders. He tended to work with cases where all previous treatments had failed.

Wetterstrand had a background in hypnosis and was familiar with most of the authorities of his time, including Bernheim and Liebault, two of the most eminent. He had some success with hypnotic treatments, and agreed with other authorities that the deeper the trance, the more likely the cure. However, he came to doubt that suggestions provided to the person in trance were the main cause of the cures. Rather, he thought, it was mainly the trance itself that healed them. In addition to depth of trance, Wetterstrand decided that the length of the trance was a major factor. He therefore began to extend the duration of somnambulistic trances to weeks and even months. His therapeutic success rate then greatly increased and he was able to succeed where all previous treatments, including hypnotic ones, had failed. He called his method Artificially Extended Sleep.

He would assign to the patients times for eating, bathing, excreting and so on, and reported that these schedules were involuntarily kept. The trance was reinforced as frequently as he thought necessary, and the patient remained in trance while sleeping in the normal way as well as while functioning as if in a waking state. It is not clear just how much time patients spent in bed, but evidently they remained there most of the day as well as night. Improvements were usually noted to occur gradually, although sometimes all at once the symptoms would disappear. The patients evidently accepted Wetterstrand's statements to them that they were sleeping and there seems to have been no exploration of trance phenomena such as images or hallucinations, if they occurred. A friend or some other trusted person would be with the patient while he or she was eating at predetermined times, and on a few other occasions, but that person was instructed never to converse with the patient since "the more undisturbed the sleep, the more happy will be the outcome."

No one else, to my knowledge, has ever for therapeutic reasons kept a person in trance for weeks and even months. No effort, so far as we know, was ever made to determine what the mental life of the patient may have been during that extraordinarily long trance. It was conceptualized by Dr. Wetterstrand as a rest cure for the nervous system of the patient. Provide the nervous system with sufficient rest and it would produce the cure.

In the ancient world, there was the practice of temple sleep. The patient, in trance, or possibly drugged, might while sleeping have been visited by the Gods who did the healing. There were variations, but a long sleep in a powerful place where the cure was strongly expected to happen: those were the essentials. Temple sleep might also have included something like mesmerism, teams of healers passing their hands directly over the surface of the body of the afflicted one, or a little above the surface of the body, stroking for many hours or even days a presumed aura or energy field extending beyond the person's body. This would induce a trance or serve to deepen the already altered state. When such methods were used, the cure was likely to occur as a "crisis," a kind of profound and dramatic seizure, after which the symptoms were gone and the person declared cured. The person would have journeyed far into Inner Space where, at some point, the body discharged the illness and, when the mind returned to its normal reality, the illness no longer existed. There is no doubt that such healings did and do occur, presently in New Age variants, with about as many explanations to account for the results as there are varieties of healers.

Beginning in the mid-1960s, and for many years, I worked with volunteer research subjects and assistants to explore ways of achieving the most profound altered states of consciousness apart from mind-altering drugs. At The Foundation for Mind Research, first in mid-Manhattan and later in Pomona, New York, Jean and I worked with sensory deprivation and sensory overload chambers, as well as other devices, to explore most especially the creative process and the possibility of introducing the mental and other tools needed for high-level and even genius-level creativity into the repertoires of those who did not naturally possess them. Later, and using many findings from this work, I increasingly shifted my emphasis to a larger spectrum of Inner Space explorations, more along the lines of my earlier research with mescaline and LSD, but without the psychedelics. That work increasingly included somnambulistic and other very deep and also prolonged trances. I was not familiar with Wetterstrand at the time, but did get some help from my studies of the work of Milton H. Erickson, a psychiatrist who had no rival in medical hypnosis.

I was doing research, but also psychotherapy, and the deep, prolonged trances had considerable therapeutic potency. I learned from Erickson that a person can be in trance while asleep as well as in what appears to be the normal waking state. I explored with volunteers, and later with some patients, trances lasting for several days and, eventually, a week. A patient would be given many aids in the environment to reinforce and deepen her or his trance.

Passing through doorways would maintain and deepen the trance, or looking at various antiquities or other works of art in the rooms of our house. The patient would go to bed while in a deep trance and awaken into a deep trance that presumably had also existed while the patient slept. Unlike Wetterstrand, and more like Erickson, I gave many suggestions about the powers of the unconscious mind, as well as the trance itself, to achieve desirable changes and healing.

The patient's unconscious, I might suggest, will be "working all the time, or as much as is necessary or likely to be fruitful, to bring about the results your conscious mind would like to have occur. That work will be ongoing while you are sleeping as well as while you are awake, and you will be in a very deep trance the entire time." There would also be some periods of active therapy, exploring symbol systems and the like, but the emphasis was on the patient's own unconscious mind bringing about healing within the context of deep, prolonged trance.

In 1958, at about two o'clock in the morning, I was sitting with Allan Lazarus, a Shreveport, Louisiana, newspaper editor, waiting in the newsroom for the morning edition of *The Times* to come off the presses. We started talking about people we would like to meet and about trying to use some ESP to bring them in. I mentioned an actress, Diane Varsi, who had been appearing on the "Playhouse 90" television series, and who had been nominated for an Academy Award for her performance in the movie *Peyton Place.* I felt unusually drawn to her. In 1982, almost a quarter century later, I received a call from an old friend, the psychologist and parapsychologist Stanley Krippner, who said that he had someone in urgent need of help and he thought I might be able to provide it. She was an actress, Diane Varsi. I don't recall if I ever had mentioned her to Stanley. Diane Varsi then called me and said that she had a pregangrenous condition of both feet and had been told that they would have to be amputated if there was no improvement in one week. She had exhausted her medical alternatives, and a friend had sent her to Dr. Krippner as someone very knowledgeable about alternative approaches. He had then suggested me. I told her to take the first plane she could get from San Francisco to New York and I would help her if I could.

Diane Varsi proved to be extraordinary in many ways, and I quickly understood what it had been that had drawn me to her. She came, she said, from a long line of witches, and her great-grandmother had taught her witchcraft telepathically while she was a small child. She then became, and remained, very psychic—something I was able to confirm. She was a mind reader, and was strongly precognitive, clairvoyant and telepathic. Like some other real psychics I have known, she was astonishingly accident- and catastrophe-prone. She said she had been attacked by entities since childhood. Her psychic abilities were such that her family and others were afraid of her. She had an endless array of physical problems that had tormented her almost since infancy. Her physician sent me more than fifty pages of her medical records and she had presented to him and previous doctors enough symptoms to fill a page or more of this book just listing them. She had managed to have prescribed for her dozens of drugs and many of her symptoms were clearly prescription drug-induced. Her doctors found her difficult to refuse, but finally would give up and pass her along to the next one. She was subject to severe epileptic seizures, often suffered such pain in her muscles and joints that she scarcely could move, and headaches so severe that she was unable to speak. She was one of those persons who can produce the symptoms of dozens of conditions. In trance, at my suggestion, she demonstrated this ability, including blisters and swellings, inflammations, pain wherever suggested and more. She was also beautiful, intelligent, witty, had a great deal of knowledge, was a fascinating conversationalist, and was likeable despite all the problems. Our staff members were captivated by her.

Diane Varsi was clearly an hysteric able to manufacture for herself almost any kind of problem, physical or mental. However, whatever their origins, her problems were real and, in this case, the surgeon was insistent that her feet needed to be amputated. She arrived on crutches, had a brace on one leg, and her feet and ankles were very swollen and discolored. We spoke for some hours while she related to me the details of her extraordinary life. I explained to her what I had in mind, and we then began to work. She was a natural somnambulist as Dr. Krippner had told me, and was extremely amenable to the idea of remaining in trance for days at a time. After the first day, she already was better. After five days, her symptoms had completely disappeared. She then went back to San Francisco.

She went to her doctor's office on crutches, tossed them aside, threw her leg brace on the floor, and danced for him. He examined her feet and found them completely healed. He was astonished and described what had happened as "a miracle," even putting that in writing for me. She had no recurrence, but returned to spend the summer with me "just in case." She assisted me in a training program in human potentials that Jean and I were teaching, and was well liked by everyone. She and I did numerous deep trances together, some of them intended to try to determine what had happened during those five days in Inner Space that had healed her. But she was amnesiac for any such details of the trance.

We remained good friends until her death ten years later, reportedly from complications of Lyme disease. She always had some problems, but never the range of physical ones she had experienced before our work together. Occasionally, she would write to me about some emotional upheavals. "I had to put my arm through a window," she wrote once, "but it was only a small window."

I personally experienced a long trance or "extended sleep" on the occasion of my fiftieth birthday. I had attached no particular importance to that birthday but awakened to find myself, for the first time in my life, severely depressed. I could not shake the depression and, a few days later, decided to travel far enough to just leave it behind. I hoped I would leave it behind somewhere in Inner Space.

I told Jean and the Foundation staff that I intended to remain in a self-induced trance for about a week and was not to be disturbed. Someone could look in on me at ten o'clock in the morning and again at five o'clock in the early evening. I asked that a sandwich and some milk be left on a table in my office at those times. Otherwise, I was absolutely not to be disturbed for any but the most extreme cause.

After a few hours, as best I can estimate the time, I found myself looking at images of dragons. Then, after a while, I could feel my own body becoming a dragon's body.

After that I was flying with the dragons, and it was an absolutely exhilarating experience.

I flew with the dragons for most of that week, and it seemed to pass extremely quickly. When the experience was over, and the trance or extended sleep was ended, the depression was completely gone and, in fact, was replaced by an unusual good cheer that lasted for some days.

In the Far Out realms of Inner Space I had found, as have others, a most satisfactory if not very well understood resolution of problems.

Plate 1

Cosmic Figure *by artist Allan Atwell, done according to ancient
Tibetan formula. The figure in the large drawing is life-sized.
If meditated upon successfully, human bodies will become transparent.
Second stage is a vision of the Void. (Page 45)*

Plate 2

Gargoyle figure found on the
Cathedral of Notre Dame de Paris. (Page 55)

Plate 3

*The author, in 1974, with an ancient black granite statue
of the Egyptian Goddess Sekhmet in its sacred space in the
Temple of Ptah at Karnak. A magical operation was perfomed to (re)open
the eyes, ears and mouth of the idol. (Page 108)*

Plate 4

The painting by Diana Vandenberg of the Goddess Sekhmet.
Sekhmet appeared to Diana for one hour daily for each of thirty days,
when the portrait was accomplished. (Page 109)

Plate 5

*Magical painting of the elephant-headed, human-bodied God Ganesh.
Damage seemed to have drained it of its power. (Page 111)*

Plate 6

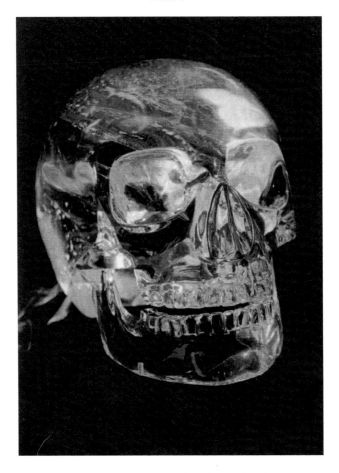

Life-sized quartz crystal skull with articulated jaw.
This is the legendary Mitchell-Hedges Skull, known also as the Skull of Doom.
It is a unique and authentic object of power. (Page 119)

Plates 7 & 8

*Vagina altar and phallic stones created by lava from
the Mauna Loa volcano of the Hawaiian Goddess Kapo. The altar accords
with the myths and legends of the Goddess and the Kapo Cavern
is surely one of the natural wonders of the world. (Pages 160 & 161)*

Plate 9

The author with Naga dragon: "What is most reassuring, after all, is the definite fact that the Dragons are in charge." (Page 169)

Chapter Fifteen

Interspecies
Communication

According to a North American Indian tradition, the famous chief Geronimo was able to talk to coyotes. He could go out onto the plain and call the coyotes and large numbers would gather before him. They would advise him about the best places to hunt and they would warn him in advance of an enemy attack.

A special relationship between a human and nonhumans—whether animals, serpents, birds or other species—is to be found in many places. Once, while in Java, I met a magician who agreed to introduce me to members of a dragon-worshipping "cult" or religion I had especially wanted to contact. These people used mind-altering plants to establish contact with the dragons. They claimed to be able to go into the only slightly more subtle and closely adjacent world of the dragons or to persuade the dragons to come into their world—something he said dragons still do on occasion, though much less often than in the past. I was unable to remain in Java long enough to participate in one of those gatherings, but he did show me something else almost equally intriguing.

I was invited to attend a ceremony where several young virgins offered their hymens to the dragons. The girls squatted over carved wooden dragons with uplifted phallic tails. These girls were first enabled to go into very deep trance states by one of the magicians, and thus their experiences of defloration appeared to be totally ecstatic and free of pain. The tails of the dragons were stained by the blood of many virgins who had made such sacrifices to them over the years.

Following this impressive ceremony, I resumed conversation with the magician who had brought me. I told him about an old Hawaiian legend of a pact made between people and sharks—the sharks being extremely numerous and savage around the islands at that time.

According to the legend, a great Hawaiian magician one day called on the chief of the sharks to come in and speak with him. A huge shark swam up to the rock where the magician was standing, and the magician then addressed that very imposing creature. He said, in effect, "We do much damage to one another. My people hunt the sharks all the time so that many of you have been killed. Similarly, you kill many of our fishermen and people who swim in the waters around our islands. I would like to propose to you that we will not hunt sharks and you will not eat people. In honor of this agreement, once each year we will sacrifice one human being to you so that you will not be false to your shark nature." The great chief of the sharks agreed and from that time onward, so the legend has it, it was extremely rare that any human being was ever attacked by a shark. In return, the Hawaiians rigidly enforced their rule against hunting sharks. Since the Hawaiians at that time engaged in human sacrifice, and sometimes in ritual cannibalism, there was no great problem about sacrificing one human being each year to the sharks. It is said that eventually the Hawaiians no longer made the annual sacrifice—although there are those who say that it is still made today.

The Javanese magician listened to this story with great interest and told me that in various parts of Indonesia there used to be people who had special relationships and pacts not only with various kinds of fishes, but also with birds and serpents. He told me that he himself had a special relationship with serpents and offered to provide a demonstration. We walked out into the jungle and there, in the bright moonlight, he fell into what appeared to be a deep trance, though it was one characterized by an exceptional alertness and extreme concentration. We stood in a clearing and after a few minutes, I began to hear rustling in the grass and brush around us. Then, as I watched with much astonishment, a variety of snakes of different sizes and colors began to move into the clearing. I was rather alarmed by this and was much relieved when they stopped six or seven feet away from us. As I looked around I saw that we were completely encircled by these different kinds of serpents. The magician spoke to them in some very curious-sounding language, spun several times in a circle, made gestures with his arms and with his legs, and then resumed his previous position, standing erect with his arms hanging at his sides. The snakes, having observed him with unwavering attention, then turned and slithered off into the jungle, disappearing as quickly and silently as they had come.

After several minutes, the magician emerged from his trance. We then talked for a while about highly developed and reciprocal telepathic connections that used to exist between human beings and animals, but that have been very largely lost. On the other hand, as we mutually agreed, it is not too difficult to reestablish telepathic communication with animals. In some cases it is present whether intended or not. In my own country, for example, many people have varying degrees of such communications with their pets, especially dogs and cats, whether they recognize it to exist or not. If such communication exists with our pets, then why not, after all, with sharks and serpents?

Chapter Sixteen

Animal Telepathy

There are innumerable accounts suggesting telepathic interchanges between human beings and animals, especially pets. Probably almost anyone who has ever had a long and close relationship with a dog or cat can recall personal examples. I have been alert for these over many years and always have tried to exclude other explanations such as the common one of suggestive "body language."

The most telepathic animals in my experience have been Old English mastiffs—one variety or another of the mastiff has been associated with humans for several thousand years. Likenesses of that breed of dog are found in ancient Egyptian art, and the Egyptians—great animal trainers and breeders—are said to have bred the mastiff to resemble the lion, which the mastiff was used to hunt. The pharaoh Ramesses II wrote a tribute to his mastiff.

My first mastiff, Titan, was an enormous beast with a head three times the size of my wife's. Before he was two years old, he developed problems with his rear legs that several veterinarians thought would condemn him to a very short life. I was told it was unlikely that even the most skilled surgery could be of help in Titan's case.

I called for assistance from my good friend, the Israeli physicist and brain scientist Moshe Feldenkrais, who had devised an extremely sophisticated method of neural and sensory reeducation. I was also working in that field. Together, we devised a way of essentially "rewiring" Titan's nervous system to reorganize his muscles and his skeleton. For months, I worked several times daily with Titan, eventually teaching him a new way to walk. That work was successful and allowed him to live for almost six more years—to a mastiff's normal life span.

From the time of Titan's recovery, he seemed to attribute God-like powers to me. When the weather was good, he would repeatedly come up to me, wag his huge tail, and cover me with kisses. When the weather was bad, he would give me such looks of reproach as only a mastiff is able to do.

My evidence for telepathy and possibly also precognition is this: Titan clearly abhorred any act of violence, especially on my part, and this extended down to me swatting a fly or stepping on a bug. At first, if I swatted a fly, Titan would go to the far corner of the room and reprimand me with his most reproachful look. Later, perhaps as his powers developed, all I had to do was *think* about swatting a fly and he would go to the corner of the room and reproach me. More than that, I could be in my kitchen, where I could observe him through a large window as he went about whatever he was doing in the dog yard. Even then, if I saw a fly, and before I could cross the room for my swatter, and no matter what he was doing or where he was looking, Titan would suddenly stop and go to the far end of the dog yard. From that distant vantage point, he would give me one reproachful look and then face away so as not to see me. This behavior happened hundreds of times and was observed by a great many people. In other ways as well, he gave persuasive evidence of telepathy and probably precognition.

My second mastiff, Queen Zingua, was equally sensitive. One psychotherapy patient who came to see me was always accompanied by two hallucinated men—one just to his left, one to his right. Zingua would always snap and snarl at the hallucinations, but never at the man himself.

Like Titan and some other dogs I have had, Zingua especially liked to be around patients and research subjects who were in deep trance. She was also very sensitive to people who were anxious or despondent, and would sit alongside such people during their therapy. They uniformly felt supported by her, and believed her to be a healing presence. Some patients even attributed to Zingua the success of their therapy!

My third mastiff, Captain Sir Richard Francis Burton, was also a telepath. As I had done to some extent with Zingua, I trained him from an early age to identify objects according to how I was concentrating on them. He could also identify images of objects that I only imagined I was holding. I would pick up, for example, a saltshaker in one hand and a teacup in the other. "Now Burton," I would say, "come and get the teacup,"' and I would focus on the hand that was holding the cup, or send him an image of the cup. It did not matter whether the object I concentrated on was familiar to him or whether he was being introduced to it for the first time.

And I was careful not to use body language that might provide him with a clue. He was successful at this about seven times out of ten, sometimes with his success rate dropping towards the end of such an "experiment," when he seemed to get bored or otherwise lose his concentration.

Eventually, however, Burton's powers of telepathy brought us to a parting of the ways. He became very sensitive to people who were thinking bad thoughts about me, and would give them warning bites. A mastiff can rip an arm from its socket, so a 250-pound Captain Burton just slightly penetrating the skin was clearly making a point and not intending to inflict any serious injury. But it became too much, the behavior could not be changed, and I returned him, with enormous regret, to the mastiff farm in Canada where he was born. There he had very large fields to roam in and no one he felt he needed to protect.

If—as it seems—some animals have better access to tele-pathic capacities than humans, then it may be that communication with images has to be developed by the animals as a substitute for language abilities, which are at best minimal. And it may be that deliberate cultivation of some kinds of imaging capacities will give humans access to telepathic faculties that exist as latent potentials in all of us.

Chapter Seventeen

Ways with Trees

My grandfather told me several times about an old man who lived in his neighborhood when he was a boy. In the old man's yard there stood a magnificent oak tree, one the whole neighborhood treasured. People from other parts of town came to look at the tree, especially when it was changing its leaves. It was said that the tree was well over one hundred years old.

For some reason the old man in whose yard the tree stood had come to hate the tree and wanted it dead. He wanted to cut it down, but his wife refused to hear of it and said the whole neighborhood would be angry if he did such an awful thing. The tree, as my grandfather recalled it, was as healthy as it was majestic, and people often talked about how it seemed to them that the tree would live at least another hundred years.

Every morning, and now and then throughout the day, the old man could be observed going into his yard and talking to the tree. He would curse the tree, sometimes strike it with a stick, or pick up a rock and hurl it against the tree's trunk. Since the tree was so enormous, it seemed impossible that it could be injured by a blow from a stick or a stone.

My grandfather remembered one day in particular when it seemed that the old man was out in the yard almost every hour cursing the tree. Then, within a very short time, the great tree sickened and died. No other tree in the neighborhood showed any signs of sickness and there was no reason anyone could think of for the tree to die—unless it was by the old man's curses.

Years later, there began to appear reports of experiments, scientifically done, describing how plants prayed over, or even just talked to in positive ways, grew larger and produced more abundantly than plants from the same source grown under conditions as identical as possible except for the prayer or encouragement. If a plant can respond to a prayer, then why not also to a curse? What bothers many people most about such reports and experiments is the implication that plants are somehow sentient. But as my old friend the philosopher Alan Watts used to say to those who considered themselves to be virtuous because they avoided eating meat: a vegetarian is just somebody who never has heard a radish scream!

I myself once knew an old farmer who claimed to understand the language of trees. He had learned it, he said, from his grandfather, and had cultivated the knowledge despite his own father's disbelief and opposition.

He said that trees, and one oak in particular, warned him of coming storms and of frosts and also told him just where and when to plant. For whatever reasons, the old farmer's green thumb and his ability to forecast the weather were phenomenal, and I profited much from his advice.

The old farmer also talked to his plants, so that neighbors thought him somewhat crazy. He, on the other hand, held that in some distant past there had been communication and cooperation between human beings and all living things that are friendly to humans—that was some, but not the whole, of living nature, since there also exist plants, animals and other creatures, some humans included, "whose business it is to do the Devil's work."

Sometimes, in this man's vicinity, it surely seemed that the leaves of the trees rustled louder, and moved more, than did those of trees nearby to which he was not listening. This was especially true of his favorite oak, the tree given to him by his grandfather to be his "teacher and friend."

Years later, I would learn that in the centuries before it was widely believed that trees warned of changes in the weather and, as well, of the coming of plagues, their leaves rustling and their branches trembling in ways that could be read by those familiar with the movements. However, it was argued by some that the trees had no special knowledge of coming weather changes. In the case of plagues, the birds simply flew ahead of the plague to warn of the direction it was taking. I wondered how much more the old man knew than he had told me? Or had he, and perhaps his grandfather as well, been deceived all their lives by duplicitous, self-aggrandizing trees? Or is there some other explanation? For the old man seemed honest to the bone, and if trees lie, then wherein shall we place our trust?

Chapter Eighteen

The Witches' Cradle

In the late 1960s and early 1970s I was especially engaged in a search for ways of inducing altered states of consciousness apart from banned psychedelic or mind-altering drugs and familiar hypnotic techniques. My research into medieval witchcraft for my book *Eros and Evil* had brought to my attention reports of a device in which witches hung suspended and immobilized while swinging to-and-fro in a pendulum-like movement. This device was called a Witches' Cradle. The body of the witch remained in the Cradle while, in an imaginal or dreamlike body, she journeyed to a gathering of witches called the Witches' Sabbat. It was evident that some kind of trance was induced by the Cradle. When her Sabbat experience had ended the witch would come out of the trance and tell whoever was attending her to release her from the device.

An engineer friend constructed for me a kind of metal swing in which a person could stand, and which was suspended from a metal frame by a length of rope. The person was strapped into the

Cradle so that there was no possibility of falling. Distractions were minimized by blindfold goggles and a sound-excluding headset through which, however, instructions could be given. The research subject was told to focus on the movements of the Cradle, generated by small muscular movements that would happen in response to whatever images were being experienced. The subject was told that some kind of altered state would soon occur and then we should be told what was happening and interaction between experimenter and subject would begin. That interaction would depend on the purpose of the session.

My wife was at the time an associate professor of philosophy at Marymount College close to New York City where we lived and the Foundation had its lab. At the time there was immense interest in altered states and the students from this Catholic girls' college were eager to participate in our work. The nun who headed the philosophy department was a good friend and fully supportive of the research and the students' participation in it.

Deep trances occurred quickly and regularly in the Cradle. At our suggestion, the girls experienced image world adventures which, in some cases, unfolded as stories that they easily turned into fiction, poetry and even philosophical essays. As word of this research got around, professors from other Catholic schools wanted to be volunteers. One rather well-known Jesuit theologian, Ewert Cousins, guided by Jean in some dozens of sessions, experienced virtually the gamut of religious and mystical experiences, and the transcripts of his tape-recorded sessions came to several hundred pages. Afterwards came swamis of Yoga, philosophers, psychologists, artists and others. Their experiences attracted attention worldwide and photographs and accounts of the work with the Cradle appeared in countless newspapers and magazines including *The New York Times*, *Time*, *Der Spiegal* in Germany, *Intellectual Digest* and so on.

We often used suggestions about "time distortion," or "accelerated mental process (AMP)," a technique researched by the great specialist in medical hypnosis psychiatrist Milton Erickson. With this approach, what seemed to be an hour or more of subjective experience could take place within one minute of "objective" clock-measured time. I had first seen this demonstrated by Erickson when, at a gathering of physicians, one doctor's wife, in trance, had the experience of going to a theater, buying a ticket, finding a seat, and then watching from beginning to end the lengthy film *Gone with the Wind*, all within just one minute. Such AMP had often occurred spontaneously in our work with the psychedelic LSD-25.

One day, brought by our friend science writer Gay Luce, there arrived at our lab for a demonstration the famous authentic World War II hero General James Gavin. Gavin had been the youngest major general in the U.S. Army since George Armstrong Custer and had led the paratroopers in the Normandy invasion. "Gentleman Jim," as he was known, had retired as a full general and at the time was president of the prestigious Arthur Little Company. He was looking for ways to make his executives more creative, and Gay had told him about the Cradle.

We gave him a preliminary briefing, strapped General Gavin into the Cradle, and sent him on his way. He appeared to go into a deep trance almost at once. Soon, however, it was obvious that he was experiencing some distress. Since his arms were immobilized at his side, he could not remove the blindfold goggles or release himself. However, he asked to get out of the Cradle, a wish with which we quickly complied. He then said something about having another appointment and very quickly left. We found out later that he had found himself in a parachute, bullets whizzing all around him, and had no desire to find out what might be the end of that experience.

Our friend, former Apollo astronaut Edgar Mitchell, known as "Sixth Man on the Moon," tried a later, horizontal version of the Cradle that allowed the person to lie down rather than stand. Mitchell had been known as the "most intellectual" of the astronauts, with a doctorate in astrophysics from M.I.T. He was also the most adventurous and intellectually curious apart from space exploration, and had created controversy by attempting an experiment in telepathy from the moon. He went on to spend his life exploring in the realms of parapsychology and human potentials.

Mitchell knew, as experiments with hypnosis prove, that a person senses more than manages to get into his consciousness. That "more" can be retrieved in trance. When on the moon, he had stood near a ridge and had felt very strongly that something important was on the other side. He had wanted to go look, but he was outranked by the other astronaut on the moon with him, Alan Shephard. Shephard ordered him not to go and Mitchell thereafter felt a great sense of frustration. He wondered if his sensory field might not have extended far enough to include real knowledge of what lay beyond the ridge, and if the fact he unconsciously possessed such knowledge might not account for the frustration he continued to feel long after he had returned to planet Earth.

Mitchell wanted me to put him in a trance and take him back to the moon where perhaps he could retrieve the hitherto inaccessible knowledge. However, test pilots are almost always impossible to hypnotize, and Mitchell was no exception. The original vertical Cradle did not work for him either. For one thing, as had happened with Gavin, he found himself in a parachute. However, with the horizontal Cradle, he finally went into trance and quickly found himself on the moon exactly where he had been before, but without Alan Shephard to forbid his exploration. He then went over the ridge, but there found only "more rocks." No mystery or discovery of importance was achieved, but it was satisfying to have another experience of walking on the moon, and he would find himself no longer tormented by the feelings of possessing inaccessible knowledge. Whatever the validity of his trance experience, it did provide that relief.

I took many journeys of my own in the Cradle, sometimes with Jean taking the role of experimenter, sometimes not. Among other things, I found I could enter into novels, experience the characters and interact with them—novels written by others, and also my own fiction. We placed two of the vertical Witches' Cradles side by side and explored the ability of people to share a common trance reality in that way. Others in various parts of the country and the world built their own versions and some found it useful for psychotherapy as well as for research. The name Witches' Cradle frightened away some of the more orthodox researchers, as did the name and acronym ASCID (Altered States of Consciousness

Induction Device). ASCID was a playful reference to the favorite mind-altering approach of the time—LSD, lysergic acid diethylamide, popularly known as acid.

The physiological effects of the Cradle were never examined. As a psychological tool, it deserves more study. As a gateway for the Inner Space explorer, it is always there and, as yet, no one has passed a law against it!

Chapter Nineteen

Mysteries of the Eye

It is an important but rather mysterious fact that the human body is equipped with more receptors directed inwards than there are receptors directed outwards. That is, we seem to be physically less well equipped to experience the external world than we are to experience Inner Space. Those visual receptors directed inwards normally go very largely unused, or at least what the visual organs may sense is not usually accessible to consciousness.

All of the senses can be used in Inner Space—in dreams, in trance and drug states, in the worlds of fantasy, mental illness, visionary experience, and in the special worlds opened up by meditation and other magical and spiritual practices. For most people, the dream world is by far the most familiar of these, and the visual sense is more commonly used in dreams than in any of the other states.

There are dream experiences of moving and touching, less often of hearing (as distinguished from just knowing what is said), and rather few experiences of smell and taste. However, all are possible. With respect to the visual sense, it has been found that color occurs in only about one-third of dreams. On the other hand, color and light are among the most important features of almost all other Inner Space experiences and, the more profound the experience, the more intense and meaningful are color and light. Dreams, having to do with aspects of everyday life, are of a different order than experiences of worlds reached by going inwards—and the senses respond differently to the images of these different realms.

The human eyes, looking inwards at visionary worlds, are able to observe more precisely and in greater detail than can the eyes looking outwards. It is possible, for example, to see clearly in Inner Space an image composed of many hundreds of smaller images, and to see all of them with equal clarity. It is also possible in Inner Space to see spontaneously and with equal clarity objects that are close-up and objects that are distant.

In altered states this beautiful curiosity of vision also happens in the case of the external world. Perspective is maintained, with close-up objects appearing to be larger than distant ones, but the detail of the distant object is as clearly perceived as is the detail seen close-up.

For example, looking out over a meadow with trees, no matter how great the distance, as far as the eye can see, every blade of grass is seen with absolute clarity and every detail of the bark of trees and their leaves. The distant bird is much smaller, but every detail of the bird is seen just as if the bird were sitting on one's hand.

With this kind of vision, or with variations of it, can occur those "dawn of creation" experiences where it seems that everything is completely new, being seen for the first time. Sometimes this happens during a religious experience and sometimes it happens with mind-altering drugs—always, it is an experience of overwhelming beauty. The same kind of thing can be seen in visionary worlds and, as Aldous Huxley once remarked, this kind of vision is reminiscent of accounts of paradisiacal worlds to be found in many times and places.

Also in the literature of religious experience, spiritual practices, and drug and trance states, there are accounts of the eyes both taking in more light, and also generating light. A person becomes able, for example, to perceive a darkened room as if the room were well lighted. This is not just a matter of the pupils dilating to take better advantage of whatever light may be present, light is also generated.

Von Helmholz, the great authority on optics, is said to have demonstrated that he could project light out of his eyes and so read the pages of a book in almost total darkness. As I myself have experienced, and as one learns from the literature of religious experience, both the light encountered in Inner Space and in the external world under darkened conditions can become so bright as to be uncomfortable or even unbearable. Then, if the light is experienced as being outside of oneself, one may have to close one's eyes to get away from the brightness. If, on the other hand, the light is perceived as coming from inside of one's self, then one may need to open one's eyes to escape it.

Sometimes this kind of light perceived in visions and in religious experiences is called "preternatural," and it conveys the impression of great beauty, sometimes also of the Holy and the Numinous. Schizophrenics describe light of comparable intensity, but it is glaring and frightening and painful—the lights of Hell as compared to those of Heaven.

The ability to see clearly in the dark is an actual seeing with the eyes, not the kind of sensing with the whole body that is cultivated in the martial arts and by some shamans. That kind of sensing allows the person, for example, to run through the woods in darkness without bumping into objects, and it is akin to the sensing of some animals—such sensing is surely a natural capacity of humans, but one that has been lost and usually only can be recultivated with great effort.

Some spiritual disciplines, such as Yoga, also claim to be able to train the eyes so that it becomes possible to see beneath the surface of objects, also beneath the surface of the earth. A Yogi sufficiently accomplished in this way has so-called "x-ray vision," and is able to see into human bodies to diagnose illness and injury.

This by no means exhausts the mysteries of the human eyes, but it provides more examples—if any were needed—of the narrow limits of our existing scientific knowledge. More importantly, these examples demonstrate clearly how small a use is presently made of human potentials, and the vast riches of experience and capacity lying untapped within all people.

Chapter Twenty

A Warning against Straining the Limits of Credulity

Once, while in India to deliver one of my lectures concerning the erotic mysteries carved on the Khajuraho Temple, I drove for several days with an Indian philosopher friend to visit a few ashrams and other points of interest.

We came to a place just outside of a village where the philosopher pointed out to me the ruins of a rather large burned-out building. He told me that the building and the land around it were in such ill repute that they could be purchased at an exceedingly low price. However, he said, no one would ever work there and builders, if any could be found, would have to be brought in from some other region. I asked him what dreadful crime or work of evil had taken place there that the place was so shunned. He then told me the following story.

A Yogi from the north of India left his home and wandered until he reached a tropical region. He then established an ashram and over a period of time acquired many pupils and followers.

The Yogi's success and popularity were great as he performed all sorts of healings and demonstrated fantastic *asanas* or Yoga postures, contorting his body in apparent defiance of normal musculoskeletal and gravitational limitations. He lectured brilliantly and convincingly concerning such human potentials as telepathy, clairvoyance, precognition, levitation, astral body travel and such still more advanced arts as becoming invisible and the creation of thought forms or visual images made material. His students worked long and hard in certainty that as a result of their labors they would eventually experience these *siddhis,* or miraculous powers, and then go beyond that to the more important and sublime experiences of *samadhi*, *nirvana* and ultimate union with the Absolute.

Neither the residents of the region nor the students ever doubted that such fruits of yogic practice were possible or that they would eventually be achieved by the Master's pupils.

Years passed and one day the Yogi spoke casually to the people concerning the place of his origin. He told the dwellers of the tropical region that, in his homeland to the north, it frequently happened that the waters of the rivers and lakes became solid and all of the people, even the most humble villagers, were able to walk upon the water.

The people were outraged at the Yogi's preposterous statement, which to them cast doubt on all of the teachings he had given to them over the years. That trained Yogis could fly or become invisible or have knowledge of future events—those claims the people could believe. But what kind of wretched liar would maintain that water is ever solid or that untrained peasants could walk on the water like wizards?

The people rose up en masse against the Yogi. His students burned the ashram. The villagers attacked the Yogi with stones, driving him from the region and teaching him the lesson that one should not overtask the imaginations of those whom one is teaching.

Chapter Twenty-one

In Search of
the Miraculous

I once knew an artist who had spent some years immersed in the lore of the magical and the miraculous, especially those mysteries found in the Far East. He was convinced that the paranormal phenomena that had always eluded his search in the West would be easy to find in India. He managed to save enough money to go to India for one year, where he planned to study art, and seek out individuals who could demonstrate extraordinary powers.

In India, he visited a great many places, making lengthy and arduous journeys. Whenever he was told of a holy man or a guru or adept supposedly able to manifest *siddhis*, or abilities usually thought to be miraculous or magical, he would trek there. In every case his efforts came to nothing. Sometimes at the end of a pilgrimage he would find only some wretched fakir, able to demonstrate nothing that was not commonplace in the streets of any large Indian city. Self-proclaimed wizards were obvious conjurers and charlatans preying upon the credulity and will to believe of whatever followers they had managed to gather.

Some who were supposed to be sorcerers told the artist that they could not demonstrate their powers for the merely curious. Since he could not persuade these sages of the seriousness of his interests and intentions, the artist had no way to evaluate their claims and so had to continue his search burdened by his ever-growing frustrations.

Finally, the time came for him to leave India. To his knowledge, not one *siddha* had he seen, nor one wizard had he encountered. Whether the supposed holy men or women were actually holy he couldn't say, and he certainly had not found the Teacher he had hoped to find to aid him in his own spiritual quest.

Ready to leave India, the artist walked down a street in Calcutta silently cursing all those who claimed to have powers beyond the ordinary. "All fakes," he muttered to himself. "Every last one of them fakes." He repeated this to himself over and over again. Suddenly, he raised his eyes and found himself gazing into the swarthy and unfriendly face of a man in a turban who stood across the street. For a moment the artist could hear his own words ringing in his ears. All at once, he felt as if he had been struck in the middle of his head with an axe. The pain was agonizing and he fell to the street losing consciousness. Later he found himself being assisted to his feet by a sympathetic passerby. The man in the turban was gone. The artist was left with what was absolutely the most terrible headache of his life. The unbearable pain persisted until he was about two days out to sea—when all at once it was gone.

The artist was excited to have what he felt was proof that what he had been seeking in the Far East really did exist. He decided that his efforts had been lacking in sufficient intensity or duration and resolved to return and renew the quest.

He did eventually return to India, and for a time lived in Nepal and Tibet as well. He found teachers, many wonders were revealed to him, and he achieved remarkable growth, spiritually, and as an artist. However, he affirmed to me that his greatest debt would always be to the man in the turban. He had needed, the artist believed, some proof that was unmistakably *real*—and no amount of skepticism or rationalization on his part could shake the authenticity of his pain!

Chapter Twenty-two

Magical Statues

In the ancient world, according to tradition, the art of making "magical statues" was well known and widely practiced. There are many surviving accounts of such statues—especially as they existed among the Egyptians, the Greeks, and a few other ancient peoples. The most famous of these statues have vanished altogether, or it may be that there still remain some fragments.

For example, at Olympia in Greece there still exists the formidable head of the once powerful "cult statue" of the Goddess Hera. According to several traditions, this statue both moved and spoke. It advised particularly on military matters and political ones, predicted the future, and also functioned as a Teacher for certain Greek philosophers.

There are other much smaller magical statues still existing in Greece—almost all Goddess figures—but they are not to be found mentioned in history books and are the property of esoteric Schools. Some of these Schools claim continuous existence since the times of the metaphysical philosophers and teachers Heraclitus, Pythagoras and Plato, respectively.

By far the greatest number of both ancient and modern magical statues still existing are to be found in India and, secondarily, Nepal—both places where the ancient Gods and Goddesses are still alive and potent for large numbers of people. There are also a great many magical images of Gods and lesser supernatural beings to be found in Indonesia, especially in Bali. Again, the Gods are still, in these places, very much alive for many people. The images are created presently by carvers and other artists claiming knowledge of how to indwell the image with something of the spirit and powers of the god represented. Tibet was once a treasure trove of magical statues, but since the Chinese occupation and persecution of religious leaders, most of the statues have been taken from the country.

In Bali, representations of the Gods, including masks, are used to produce trance-possession states, allowing the person possessed to take on some of the powers of the god. For example, men possessed by the monkey-headed God Hanuman are able to run up the trunks of trees as probably no human can do apart from such a state.

In Egypt, in the Temple of Ptah at Karnak, there is a large standing black granite statue of the ancient lioness-headed, human-bodied Goddess Sekhmet that has acquired a great reputation in recent decades for providing paranormal experiences to many who visit the temple (Plate 3). The phenomena include seemingly verifiable knowledge of previously unknown past events and present distant events, healings both physical and psychological, and access to various psychic and creative capacities hitherto latent. Many, in the presence of this formidable statue of Sekhmet, feel "seized" by the Goddess—an experience the ancient Egyptians called *hanu*—after which she may appear to them in dreams and visions and direct them to seek out her Path. Since I am the author of a book about Sekhmet, many such persons find their way to me with questions about what to do. If they are artists, they feel the need to re-create Sekhmet's image as she has appeared to them.

One particularly remarkable example is a painting of Sekhmet done by my good friend the Dutch artist Diana Vandenberg, painted after she visited and was "seized by" a three thousand-year-old idol of the Goddess (Plate 4). Every morning for one month, at the exact same time, Diana experienced a spontaneous trance and then, for one hour, Sekhmet appeared before her and "sat for her portrait." Such trances were unique in Diana's experience and the painting is, so I believe, probably her most powerful. I might add that she has been described as the finest Dutch painter since Rembrandt.

There are now an astonishing number of sites on the Internet—some thousands—where Sekhmet is the subject of discussion. A worldwide religious movement appears to be forming, or already has to some extent formed, rooted in people's experiences of several magical statues and other images of the goddess, including the Sekhmet statue in the Temple of Ptah.

In India, where there are many magical statues of Gods and Goddesses, there are also many statues of the Buddha that are used for magical purposes, especially by Tantrics. Of the Gods, there are more statues of the elephant-headed, human-bodied God, Ganesh, than of all the others put together. Of the Goddesses, the largest number of statues are of Kali, a violent and powerfully sexual manifestation of the Great Mother as both Love Goddess and Destroyer—and there are surely more *magical* statues of Kali than of all the other Gods, Goddesses and Buddhas combined.

In 1996, Western newspapers told of strange events occurring around a statue of Ganesh. Someone had been holding a container of milk in the vicinity of this statue, and the milk flew from the container to the mouth of the God. The news spread and many people began bringing milk to that statue of Ganesh with the same result. Thousands of people witnessed this phenomenon, and Indian scientists quite implausibly tried to suggest that there was something about the statue's physical composition that "attracted the milk" rather as a magnet will attract metal.

This reminded me of something I experienced while in Varanasi, an Indian city renowned for the great number of magicians who live there. A well-known astrologer in Varanasi had insisted on doing a chart for me and then was so taken with my chart that he offered to help me in any way he possibly could while I was in the city.

I spoke to him of my fascination with the pot-bellied drunken God Ganesh. According to his myth, Ganesh had become aware that the moon was a living entity and that it vampirised, or otherwise fed on, the souls and minds of humans while they were sleeping. One night, while drunk as usual, Ganesh became so angry about this that he broke off one of his elephant tusks and threw it at the moon. It stuck there, he was unable to retrieve it, and so images of Ganesh almost always show him with one missing or broken-off tusk.

The astrologer offered to take me to a School containing a special statue or idol of Ganesh. It was quite a long walk and we passed through several places where large stacks of corpses were burning and black-robed Tantric magicians were circling the pyres. They went there to inhale the smoke from the burning bodies and thus gather *mana* (power) from the dead.

At the school, I was able to see the Ganesh figure only briefly and after much argument between the astrologer and one of the magicians. The figure of the God was about four feet in height, and I felt that I could both see and hear its breathing. The astrologer told me that it sometimes shifted its weight from one foot to the other, but that I did not see. However, to be in the presence of this idol of Ganesh was to be flooded with feelings of rapture and a sense of what is known in the literature of religious experience as the Awe-ful and the Wholly Other. Such feelings cannot be conveyed by means of words. They are ineffable and are experienced only in the presence of the authentically Numinous.

The astrologer kept tugging at my arm, insisting that we had to leave, and also insisting that I ask Ganesh for whatever I might want. I could not bring myself to do that since it seemed to me that I might thereby make some kind of commitment to the God.

Several days later, still in Varanasi, I was offered a most remarkable painting of Ganesh, which I felt had some of the properties of the idol, although it certainly was not so powerful (Plate 5). This painting was offered to me in the hotel lobby where the astrologer worked, and at a price so low I could surely not refuse it. When I showed it to the astrologer, he assured me that it was a most important magical painting and Ganesh must want me to have it.

Rather than ship the painting, I decided to carry it with me, and the astrologer assured me that I could safely roll it up in a soft cloth and carry it protected in my suitcase. Unfortunately, the painting—which seemed to be quite old—was damaged in the process. There were several large cracks across its surface, and the damage seemed to have drained it of its force. No doubt it can be repaired by someone who understands how to deal with such objects and then once again be a gateway to the magical and spiritual Path of the God Ganesh.

It is believed that the ancient magical statues were made by persons possessed of a knowledge of cosmic laws prescribing the means of their creation, and that such knowledge now has been lost. Remnants of the knowledge remain, as in Bali, but the power residing in the image created today is much less than it was in ancient times.

I have traveled over much of the world seeking out magical statues, idols, objects of power, objective works of art (Gurdjieff's term), and the like. It is my belief that whatever their other potencies, such objects have the ability to reach down into the unconscious mind and bring up physical and mental capacities not previously accessible. These objects are especially potent gateways to Inner Space, the collective unconscious, and the worlds of archetypes and supernatural beings—Powers and Principalities normally excluded from the ordinary everyday world of the reality consensus. Some of the objects induce recognizably altered states of consciousness, ranging from the rather slight to the profound. Some are best approached with the help of mind-altering drugs or trance states if they are to yield the most powerful and complete experiences. However, when such "aids" are used there is always the risk of muddying the waters, introducing into the experience elements that are extraneous and that dilute or otherwise distort the purity of what the object has to offer. The object alone, if sufficiently potent, as effectively as possible represents what Carl Jung described as an "essentially irrepresentable energy constellation," or archetype.

Chapter Twenty-three

Supernatural Art

In present day China and Taiwan (and dating back to times unknown), there is a practice known as "spirit painting." There are variations of this spirit painting, but it usually involves direct communication between the old Chinese Gods and a trance medium-artist. Since the communication is with the Gods and not with the dead, this is already quite different from the Western Spiritualism familiar in this country and Europe.

The paintings produced by the artists are usually oracular responses to questions put to the medium by his client. The painting provides an answer to the question, but that answer usually is not apparent to a client and requires interpretation by the medium.

Extremely remarkable is the manner in which these paintings are done. The artist sits with his brushes and paints in front of him. After a time he goes into trance and becomes possessed by a god. Then the brush is taken up by the opposite hand from the one that the artist would normally use: if he is right-handed, he will paint with his left. The paints are mixed very quickly, and both the mixing of the paints and the actual painting of the complex and detailed picture are done in three to five minutes. The colors are the very delicate and subtle ones so often found in Chinese painting, and it is said that there has never lived any artist who, without the help of a god, could mix paints and then execute a painting so quickly.

In Taiwan presently there are two physician-mediums, a father and a son, who carry on this tradition and have added an important dimension to it. Not only do they do the paintings as described—paintings of very high artistic quality—but the medium, having received the information from the Gods, also provides a diagnosis and a prescription for treatment of the patient who solicits the painting. A book of these paintings, magnificent as well as miraculous, has been published and contains fine photographs of many of them, as well as god-directed calligraphy. Titled *Spirit-Calligraphy and Painting*, it is published by The Society for Spirit-Calligraphy and Painting of the Orthodox School, Taipei (1995).

In the classic tradition of spirit painting, a medium will work for three to four hours, executing in that time period several dozen paintings responsive to the questions and needs of many different clients and patients. To my knowledge, there are no similar artists, although there are trance mediums who maintain that their bodies are used by the spirits of dead artists. Sometimes the work has a fairly strong resemblance to that of the spirit who is supposed to be doing the painting. However, in no case have I seen works of art

equal in quality to those of the Chinese mediums, and none accomplished with such remarkable speed, let alone with the work
being done by a hand and arm that is otherwise never used to paint
or draw, or even to write.

As concerns the technique of the mediums, I once observed
something similar with a young woman who was a student of mine
at the time. She would sit down with a sketch pad, spontaneously
go into trance, and begin to draw. She did many different kinds of
drawings, but the example I am going to describe is a typical one.
I might add that she was quite accomplished at drawing, although
not a professional artist.

Her right hand would take up the pencil and begin to draw
one-half of the head and body of a woman quite angelic in appearance and looking rather like the artist herself. That drawing would
be done at a normal rate. Then, her left hand would seize the pencil and, drawing with extreme rapidity, would fill in the other half
of the drawing, but with a face and form as demonic as the other
side was angelic. Moreover, this left hand, moving so quickly that
it was almost a blur, would make little drawings within the main
drawing—faces of terrified children, demons and many grimacing
monsters.

Sometimes, no sooner had she picked up the pencil with her
right hand—the one she would normally use—than the left hand
would snatch the pencil and, in less than a minute, execute a drawing of what appeared to be herself as a demon or kind of evil angel.

My good friend Moshe Feldenkrais observed this while he
was a guest in our house. He had written a book, *Body and Mature
Behavior,* which in his opinion demonstrated that the human mind

could be described without resorting to the notion of an "unconscious," and that bringing in the "unconscious" contributed nothing of real value to psychology. When he saw this young woman's performance, however, he revised his thinking. The conscious mind alone, exercising voluntary control of the nervous and musculoskeletal systems, could not perform what he had observed. At my suggestion, and that of my then student and also good friend anthropologist Margaret Mead, Moshe went off to try to learn more from psychiatrist Milton Erickson, regarded by both Margaret and me as having an unrivalled working knowledge of trance and the unconscious. Moshe, then in his seventies, was himself possessed of an almost certainly unrivalled practical knowledge of brain function and how to change it to overcome a vast range of problems. Nonetheless, his was a wonderfully open mind, always ready to learn something new even when the new knowledge might overturn strongly held and long-standing beliefs.

I have worked with many artists to try to duplicate the speed with which the mediums and the young woman just described were able to work. However, even when using the hand that was normally used, they could not begin to approximate what had occurred in the examples just mentioned. What happens in those cases is the result of unconscious mechanisms and processes brought into use by means as unknown to the artists themselves as to those who would like to understand and make use of them. It cannot be excluded that, in fact, and as spirit painters insist to be the case, nonhuman entities are interacting with the artists to make possible their works.

Chapter Twenty-four

Crystal Skull Mysteries

Of all the authentic power objects accessible to the seeker at the present time, none is so remarkable as the one usually referred to as the Mitchell-Hedges Crystal Skull or, sometimes, Skull of Doom (Plate 6). The first name refers to its owner or custodian, Anna Mitchell-Hedges; the second, to stories of death and other catastrophes that have occurred to people who have endangered the Crystal Skull or "aroused its wrath."

The Skull is life-sized, with an articulated jaw bone, thus differentiating it from other crystal skulls of indeterminate age and origin to be found in museums in London and Paris. Even more is it differentiated, however, by the unrivalled quality of the workmanship and by the uncanny impression it makes on those who come into contact with it. The Skull is renowned throughout much of the world and has been visited by thousands of people of every level of knowledge. Theories of its origins abound, and crystallographers doubt that there is anyone now who could duplicate the

quality of its craftmanship even with the most advanced tools. The highly skilled contemporary crystal carver Carey Robbins of Bend, Oregon, has carved beautiful skulls, which, in some respects, are at a similar level artistically. But neither he nor any of the other artists now carving crystal skulls has found the optical, and probably more arcane, secrets that set the Mitchell-Hedges Skull apart from all others.

Since crystal cannot be dated, the age of the Mitchell-Hedges Skull could only be determined by breaking it open and dating some bits of water trapped inside. Thus, the truth about its age may never be known. Occultists and psychics and others are of the belief that the Skull is from Atlantis. Some have suggested that it is the famous "head" supposedly worshipped by the Knights Templar. Others believe it to be ancient Egyptian, Mayan, or even from another planet. What is certain is that it is an extraordinary object capable of engendering extraordinary responses in almost every person who encounters it.

In my case, what I experienced was—apart from a sense that this was something absolutely special and unique—an endless procession of images, observed especially when looking at the Skull from above. The images were of ceremonies, processions, rituals and other events, usually involving large numbers of people. Sometimes these took place out of doors, sometimes inside great temples or churches. The flow of the images never stopped.

Many visitors heard the Skull speak, always to each one in his or her own language. Once, when I was present, there were seven people from seven different countries in the room and the Skull was heard by each to speak in that person's own language. All of this happened simultaneously and the voice was heard by each one as if it were spoken inside the person's head rather than into the space of the room.

Because of the fact that the jaw is carved separately from the head, it is thought that the Skull was probably an Oracle and that some method was used to make the jaw move while the Skull was speaking. It is also carved in such a way as to suggest that it was probably placed over a box containing a candle so that various lighting effects were thereby achieved. The speculations concerning the Skull are very numerous and it may be that none of the real answers concerning its origin, purpose or history will ever be found.

There are a number of other crystal skulls of unknown origins in existence, some in the hands of private collectors and some belonging to occult and mystical Orders and esoteric Schools. These skulls can be found on every continent and in at least twenty countries. Of those that have been described, it seems clear that they differ a good deal in quality of workmanship and in the effects they produce on those who encounter them. They range in size from what would be the skull of an infant to that of an adult human and there is one crude specimen considerably larger than the size of a human skull. In the last several years there has come to be a significant demand for moderately priced crystal skulls, so that ones of all sizes have recently been made for commercial reasons alone and are easily available.

There are many legendary crystal skulls, with any present whereabouts unknown, including whole clusters of them. An American Indian tradition speaks of a "Council" of twelve crystal skulls. A similar group exists in a Tibetan tradition, with some claims to the effect that those skulls still exist today in a hidden monastery. These clusters of skulls are said to have been used to control the fate of nations and even of the world, and it has been suggested that the Chinese invasion, conquest and occupation of Tibet was really motivated by the objective of taking possession of the twelve crystal skulls, which, the Chinese Communist rulers, convinced by magicians, believed would help China achieve world domination.

The most mysterious and extraordinary crystal skull of all exists, so far as is known, only in legend. There is a tradition that this crystal skull was in the possession of the very ancient and powerful Shir-zahd Order. That Order, in its original form, existed at least three thousand years ago and was dedicated to the magical and spiritual disciplines of the Goddess Sekhmet. The name of the Order means "lion-born," and is a reference to the Great Mother Goddess Sekhmet.

The Shir-zahd Crystal Skull was as perfect in execution as the presently unrivaled Mitchell-Hedges Crystal Skull. The tradition has it that the Skull replicated that of an actual god who took human form in ancient times. The Skull was carved from an enormous, perfectly clear, and otherwise flawless piece of quartz crystal and was eight or nine times the size of an adult human's skull. Like the Mitchell-Hedges Skull, it had an articulated jaw carved from the same piece of crystal. It functioned as an Oracle, actually speaking to those who had audiences with it. This included visitors from many different places and the Skull always spoke to the visitor in that person's native tongue, no matter how obscure. (This tradition was almost certainly unknown to those who experienced similar phenomena with the Mitchell-Hedges Skull.)

Not only did the Shir-zahd Crystal Skull speak, but it also functioned as a scrying, or gazing, crystal. In it could be seen images of past, present, and future events. The beholder might also receive important visions—a god, or a goddess, or some other non-human being might appear in the crystal. It is said that this Crystal Skull granted special magical and spiritual powers to certain people. It was also a major vehicle of Initiation, revealing mysteries and assigning tasks.

It was as a tribute to this Crystal Skull that Shir-zahd Teachers adopted the practice of having exact replicas of their own skulls made after death—with these replicas then being made available to special students and disciples. In the beginning, these replicas were made of different substances—wood, stone and various metals among them. In later times, it became a practice to have a mold made, and the skulls were then cast in bronze. By means of these skulls, it was said, the student could continue to learn from the Teacher until the student's own death. The skulls were not functional for anyone except the persons designated to receive them.

Three thousand years ago or earlier, the Shir-zahd Order also was reported to possess a beautifully made and spiritually powerful crystal Dragon—sometimes indwelled by a living Dragon in the manner that an idol is indwelled by a god. This Dragon was at least as large as the Skull and was also made of flawless crystal. The Dragon was said to have been of great help to the Order, particularly in three areas: ensuring victory in wars, procuring great wealth, and providing means of securing extraordinary sexual pleasures.

The Shir-zahd Order was said to possess a whole treasure house of wondrous crystal objects that were extremely useful for magic, alchemy and spiritual development. Some of those objects still belong to the Order today, but the most important ones—and especially the great Crystal Skull and Crystal Dragon—either have ceased to exist or have been hidden away. They are spoken about only in terms of the remote past. The Order still holds to the practice, in some cases, of having made and of working with the bronze skulls of extraordinary Teachers.

My interest in crystal skulls and their history and legends was an extension, first of all, of an interest in gazing, or scrying, crystals—crystal balls—and particularly in one that was reputed to have belonged to the infamous "Bloody Countess" Elizabeth Bathory, accused of countless crimes of witchcraft and sorcery, and condemned to death by the Inquisition. The crystal ball had been acquired by Heinrich Himmler and presented by him as a gift to the second in command to Adolf Hitler, Herman Goering. I was working in the Occupation of Germany and had access to the crystal. I had tried crystal-gazing in the past, but had seen nothing. In this case, however, there were images of demons and of what I took to be the Countess Bathory engaged in practices which, when later I studied her history, seemed as if they might have been images of actual past events. I was unable to pursue this particular crystal-gazing but it awakened in me a desire to explore the matter further.

Some twenty years later, having read about the Mitchell-Hedges Skull and that people saw images inside it, my wife Jean Houston and I arranged to pay Anna Mitchell-Hedges a visit at her home in Ontario and spend some time with the Skull. When I saw it I recognized the Skull at once to be the most unusual and potent of all the objects of power I had sought out in many different parts of the world. We visited Anna and the Skull on several occasions, spending many hours with it. Unfailingly it provided the processions, rituals, ceremonies, and other images I had seen on my first encounter with it. I felt that these were actual events, but was unable to comprehend their meaning. They were of another time and place and I observed them as a stranger.

Crystals enable those gifted to so use them to bring up images from the personal unconscious, including long-forgotten persons and events, and in some cases repressed memories. They also, I believe, can enable access to what Jung called the collective unconscious of the human race, or perhaps just that part of the human race to which a person has a racial connection. There are some other tools, such as "magic mirrors," that seem to do the same. Drugs and trance states can yield similar and possibly identical images. With the Mitchell-Hedges Skull, however, the impression was of something quite different that was happening. It seemed that the Skull had somehow been programmed, and that the images came from within the Skull itself, and not that it was a vehicle for bringing up images from the mind of the beholder, whether from the personal or the collective unconscious. That was at the heart of the power and mystery of the Crystal Skull. The carvers—and it is thought the Skull probably took generations to produce—had to understand how to make it a suitable vehicle for such programming, and someone had to know how to introduce the program. I should guess there is knowledge of great importance in that program, but will anyone ever have the opportunity to discover what is there?

Chapter Twenty-five

Power and Its Perils

Most esoteric disciplines require that the student demonstrate a complete obedience to the Teacher in all things. This is held to be essential for many reasons, some of them doubtless good and some specious, but there can be no doubt that this practice can make the life of the Teacher much easier.

In some disciplines, as in Zen Buddhism for example, any mistake by the student is noted by the Master who promptly strikes the student with a stick. This may go on for years until the student becomes advanced enough to teach. He then acquires a stick of his own along with some students. Similarly, in Yoga there is a saying: "If your Guru curses you, it is a blessing. If your Guru strikes you, it is a caress."

A real advantage of the Guru system is that it allows the Teacher to rid himself, with minimal discomfort, of undesirables. It is a common practice, for instance, for the Teacher to send a student to sit in a cave for thirty days while meditating and living on a diet of bread and water or some similar spartan fare. Or the student may be banished to a platform on a pole, or in some primitive cultures, placed in a bag and left to dangle from a tree limb for several days or even longer. These practices can be beneficial to the student, and they have their real uses in very rigorous training methods. However, as the late renowned magus Aleister Crowley once freely admitted, they are even more valuable as means of simply ridding oneself of undesirables.

Teaching in such a tradition, I once had a student dig a grave-like hole in the ground, put a cover over it, and remain there in darkness for a week, being only brought occasional water to drink, and briefly emerging to relieve herself. I sent her there because she was a pest. However, at the end of the week, she came to me and requested to be allowed to return and spend a second week in the hole. I agreed to this, and one week later she announced that her life had been transformed, that many of her problems had been solved, and that she had attained a degree of enlightenment. It was, she said, the greatest experience of her life, and she could not possibly thank me enough for having allowed her to do it. In fact, what she said appeared to be true, and she achieved more in the hole than she had achieved in several years of psychoanalysis and an equal amount of time practicing Yoga, not to mention one month of intensive study with me.

I could end on this happy note, but it also is necessary to sound a warning against undue exploitation of the pupil by the Teacher. A Master of Shao Lin Temple Boxing once told me the story of another Chinese Master who had an obnoxious student of whom he wanted to rid himself. The Master took the student out into the forest in the center of which stood a very large tree. The Master told the student that he must rise early each morning and begin to strike the tree with his fists, doing so for as long as he was able to endure doing it. He would become able, as time went by, to strike the tree for longer and longer periods and also with more vigorous blows. Only when, by this means, he had killed the tree should he return to again study with the Master.

Almost ten years elapsed before the student became so powerful that, in fact, he beat the great tree to death. When the tree was definitely dead, he returned and presented himself before the Master, announcing that his assignment was completed. The Master was skeptical and demanded that the man bring him and the other students to see the tree. This was done, and after he had shown the tree to the Master, the student killed the Master with one blow, taking over the School. This tale should serve as a warning to all Gurus—who should temper their self-interest with some prudence.

Chapter Twenty-six

The Tantric Ashram

M y friend and sometime teacher Swami Karmananda described to me some of his experiences in a Tantric ashram where the students were taught about sexual energy and practices as the Way to spiritual and magical development. He applied for admission when in his late teens, and first was given a very thorough physical examination. It had to be established that his body had no blemish or deformity. It was also required that he had previously mastered a number of *asanas*, or Hatha Yoga physical postures.

When he was accepted into this esoteric School his head was immediately shaved. Then, on the first night, he was led to the door of a totally darkened room and cautioned that no word should be spoken. Inside, he discovered, were many other residents of the ashram. All were completely naked, as he was, and collective sexual activity was in progress.

In the total darkness and total silence, it was impossible to know the identity of one's partner. The shaved heads could also reveal nothing. As he soon learned, a very great variety of sexual practices were engaged in, and with members of both sexes. Overcoming inhibitions was an especially important part of this phase of the work.

These gatherings were held every night, and apart from that no sexual activity was permitted. This had the effect of preventing erotic attachments between individuals—attachments that might have fostered exclusivity and prevented the required complete sharing.

Although at this stage the young male initiates had not yet learned to prevent emission of semen, something they would master later on, so far as he could tell the females never became pregnant. It was said that the spirits of the temple prevented conception.

During the sex, which progressed over time in both duration and intensity, a collective consciousness, very ecstatic, was generated by the free and passionate indulgence of the youthful initiates. It seemed that all of the bodies and minds became one in a throbbing, frenzied union.

The swami imparted to me many usually strictly guarded Tantric techniques for seduction and sexual magic, but swore me to absolute secrecy concerning them—although they could be disclosed to serious, advanced students. However, the reasons for engaging in certain kinds of sexual practices for spiritual development is not secret and is found in many systems—Tantric, Taoist and Western sex magic among them.

A primary goal is the strengthening of neural pathways, and the creation of new ones, so that the body is not consumed by the intense sensations that need to continue uninterrupted for many hours if a transformative energy such as *Kundalini* is to be experienced without risk of madness or death. Students of such practices are enabled to experience, throughout the whole body, orgasm without climax lasting for hours. This prolonged sexual ecstasy not only alters the nervous system but provides experiences of profoundly altered states of consciousness, including mystical union. These altered states give access to a variety of potentials that are usually only latent—paranormal abilities being among them.

As with the practices of other kinds of esoteric Schools, great discipline and strenuous application are required if such results are to be at last obtained. Thus only a few reach the higher levels of the work and achieve all or almost all of what is possible.

Chapter Twenty-seven

A Tale from Tibet

A Tibetan lama told me of a monk who found himself in a most difficult situation. The monk had come to know of a great female Saint, a holy woman of very high development in just those spiritual matters with which the monk himself was concerned. He felt that even a single conversation with this exemplary lady could spare him many years of arduous work.

However, the monk had already labored for years to purge himself of any vestige of sexual desire. To maintain this complete celibacy of mind-body-spirit, he had gone to dwell in a cave where no woman was allowed to set foot. He was fearful that the sight of the opposite sex would be more than he could take, and that lust would rise up to undo him.

Year after year, the monk grappled with the problem, torn between his need to speak with the holy woman and his fears that the sight of her would stir carnal thoughts. He meditated on this dilemma for five years, then ten years, then twenty. He was growing old and he finally sensed one day that sexual desire was all but dead within him. Having waited another year to confirm this, he sent word to the lady requesting he be given an audience. Another year passed before his message could be delivered and her reply returned to him. It was favorable: she would be very pleased to speak with him. The monk at once made preparations for his journey.

When at last he reached the temple where she lived, was brought inside and led to the door of her room, anxiety once again seized him. Suppose his desires were not really extinct? Suppose impure urges should arise in him? However, the monk had waited so long, and his need for the holy woman's wisdom was so great, he determined that he would risk everything.

He walked into the room where she sat on an elevated platform. When she saw him, the Saint, who despite her years looked radiantly youthful, smiled and slowly, deliberately pulled open her gown, exposing herself to the waist.

When she did this, the monk perceived that her body was invisible—so pure as to be immaterial or too subtle to be sensed. "See," she said to him, "there never was anything for you to fear."

Chapter Twenty-eight

Astronauts, Divers and Dolphins: A Fatal Rapture

Skin divers, when they go down very far, experience something called the Rapture of the Deep. They are seized by an incomparable feeling of freedom, a euphoria that swells to become bliss so overwhelming that the diver no longer is conscious of anything but his intense craving to go even deeper, and so experience more. If, at this time, there is mobilized a powerful, survival-oriented counterforce, then he is able to pull back. Otherwise, he ecstatically descends into the embrace of Death.

Astronauts on "space walks" also experience this rapture. Floating in space, attached to the ship by a cord, they describe a powerful and almost irresistible yearning to sever the cord and go drifting, drifting out into the vastness around, savoring the rapture. Out there somewhere, the body in the space suit would die, then describing endless orbits. Fellow crewmen must pull the astronaut back, depriving him of eternity to give him time.

In the early days of LSD research, several times the drug was administered to dolphins—beings with brains that suggest they may be more intelligent than humans are, although it is an alien and as yet very largely unfathomable mind the dolphin has. But the dolphins, having been given LSD, seemed to experience something akin to the diver's rapture of the deep, or the ecstasy of astronauts drifting in space. The dolphins, as described, wore expressions of bliss as, surrendering to their experiences, they simply sank beneath the surface of the water, there to drown.

Once an enormous dose of LSD was given to an elephant, with very different results—panic, convulsions, death. The opposite end of the spectrum—Hell, not Heaven—seemed to be what the elephant experienced.

And so, it would seem, both for man and for others, there are dimensions of experience that draw consciousness beyond the outer limits of its resiliency, until it snaps. We venture too far and we die, of pleasure or of pain. Whether, in such a case, it matters what the condition of our dying may have been, is a question to consider.

There is another point that is, to me, of great interest here. As I know from personal experience, it is possible to reeducate, and to some extent recreate, the human body and mind so that they can accept experiences of rapture and bliss and ecstasy that would overwhelm the body-mind in the absence of such specialized work. There are several ways of achieving such reeducation and re-creation, but the most accessible ways involve working with sexual energy, as in Tantric or some other sex magical practices.

Not only do the brain, the nervous system, and the senses become able to experience durations and intensities of pleasure that would have previously resulted in "burnout" and disastrous consequences for body, mind or both, but the sex magical practices actually create new neural pathways in the body. There are corresponding changes in the brain, in the tactile sense and other senses, and also at still more subtle levels. By means of all of these changes, a person's pleasure capacities are immeasurably increased.

Should we consider such practices as a way of "inoculating" divers and astronauts? But then what do we do about dolphins?

Chapter Twenty-nine

The Assistant of Death

A physician once told me that during a war, and before he had studied medicine, he was faced with the seemingly insoluble problem of trying to give some kind of help to mortally wounded Pakistani soldiers. He spoke only English, which most of them did not speak.

On the battlefield, where many lay dying in agony, he experienced a terrible anguish and a feeling of helplessness. He desperately wanted to ease the pain of the wounded soldiers, but he had no means to accomplish this. Then a very curious inspiration suddenly came to him.

He cradled a mortally wounded man in his arms and held him for a little while, gently, and with the intention of giving the man comfort. Then, gradually, he found himself starting to breathe in rhythm with the dying man. He deliberately cultivated this rhythm and maintained it for several minutes. Then, without at first knowing why he was doing that, he held his breath for as long as he could. Then the soldier's breathing also stopped, and very soon he was mercifully dead.

Many, many times, this man told me, he repeated that same act, and each time brought the release of death to a mortally wounded, suffering man.

Years later, this man, who became a physician, still is baffled by that strange experience. Was it the right thing to do—to help those soldiers to die? He now feels certain that in fact it was right, although for many years he had some doubts. What perplexes him most is the source of the knowledge that came to him about how to terminate the soldiers' suffering. To say that the knowledge was born of anguish, of desperation, explains nothing. It seems to him that the anguish did somehow summons the source of the knowledge. But what was the Source?

This man's story reminds me of experiences described to me by surgeons who may have experienced that Source. It spoke to them during an operation when the life of a patient was in very grave danger. It happened when a surgeon had reached the limits of his knowledge. Then "Something" spoke to him—sometimes audibly, sometimes silently—imparting a knowledge he did not have before. Then the surgeon, if he acted on this knowledge, transcended any of his known capacities, and did the thing that saved the patient's life.

Sometimes this Source speaks to other physicians, not just surgeons. When they have exhausted all resources afforded by their training, a "voice" makes itself known to them, saying: Admit that you cannot save this patient. Recognize that your best efforts have not been enough, and in full humility now simply ask that the necessary help be given to your patient. In many cases, when the doctor is able to do this, his or her patient has made what seems to be a "miraculous" recovery.

The Source in these cases may be the unconscious mind. It may be Something else. In any case, the person who experiences this Source recognizes that it knows more than he knows, and that it can enable him to achieve more than he could ever do without its guidance. Invariably, this Source is experienced while occurring as *mysterious*. Later, the physician may invent various explanations less threatening to the self-image of a scientist.

It does seem that the letting go of Self, the opening to and heeding what is offered by a Source perceived to be providing authentic information, can result in achievements otherwise impossible. That Source, unknown to the person informed by it, is a mystery not yet adequately explainable.

Chapter Thirty

Exceptional Exits

It is often exceedingly difficult for disciples or students of a Saint, or Guru or other great Teacher to accept that the Teacher, no matter how advanced, is a human being and will die. But the Teacher always does die, and that cannot be denied. Then, there must be something very different about how the Teacher dies. It cannot be the same kind of death as that of an ordinary man or woman.

Gurdjieff, almost certainly the greatest Teacher to appear in the West in this century, was quoted as saying: "I not die. I Gurdjieff." Nonetheless, he did die and the place where his corpse was buried is marked by two large stones just outside of what was once his Institute for the Harmonious Development of Man in Fontainebleau, France. I have been there, sat by those stones one evening, and drank a bottle of calvados—a favorite drink of his, as it is of mine—in his honor. At his death, Gurdjieff was attended by a young American physician, William Welch, who was one of his students. Dr. Welch, who came to reside in New York City, wrote a book and, describing the event, said that he had seen many men die, but the death of Gurdjieff was quite unlike any other. He does not explain how, and I tried in vain for years to get him to not just leave the matter hanging with that kind of statement. Not even his wife, Louise, who also had studied with Gurdjieff, could persuade him, although she agreed with me that an explanation was warranted. If she knew the details, she would not divulge them, and he offered not so much as a hint, evidently taking his secret with him to the grave.

In the Far East, it is not only in Tibet that some Saints and other very holy persons are said to grow smaller as death approaches, leaving the world, by some accounts, at the very same size as they entered it. The phenomenon is reported also in India, and there are other accounts according to which the Guru's body dwindles down to the size of an intermingled ovum and sperm and then dematerializes altogether.

Swami Karmananda described to me a process known as *Kaya Kalpa* that he said allows a very advanced Yogi to simply shed his old body at death and then at once reincarnate, acquiring a new one. There are variations in the way this can occur and sages speculate that *Kaya Kalpa* may explain the resurrection of Jesus Christ. In the case described—which my friend had not witnessed, but believed to be authentic—when an old swami was ready to die, he gathered other Yogis around him. Like many old holy men, this one had acquired an enormous belly, rather like that of the elephant-headed God Ganesh.

 The swami caused a large fire to be built, sat down next to it, and extruded from his mouth a long narrow piece of a white substance. Taking hold of one end of it, he pulled it out until it was long enough to cut into three pieces. He began chanting and praying and dropped one piece into the fire. He chanted and prayed some more and then dropped the second piece into the fire. The third piece, however, he only held close to the fire, then took it into his mouth and ate it.

After that, he sat while his already huge belly got bigger and bigger and finally burst open. Out of the empty space thus created stepped a beautiful young boy who picked up what was now the corpse of the old swami and tossed it onto the fire. The boy then departed from the place, evidently to make a new life for himself.

Under most circumstances, any properly accomplished practitioner of an authentic psychospiritual discipline ought to at least be able to choose the time of his or her death and achieve it without very much suffering or other difficulty. The death should be approached in about the same way anyone would behave in executing an orderly job of moving out of a house. Leaving the house, one would shut off the water, electricity and gas, closing down any other systems that might still be in operation. In the case of dying, the person should have learned how to be able to turn off his or her heart and then brain, having already attended to whatever else might be necessary to accomplish a quiet and graceful departure. In this way, the dying is done with the least possible disruption of the lives of others, and the soul, if the person possessed one, hopefully will be tranquil as it voyages to whatever may be its next destination.

The kind of death just described should be the norm, and surely the time will arrive when most people will have learned to be in sufficient command of their own minds and bodies to self-terminate by making use of that self-mastery when it seems to be appropriate.

I have seen a number of men and women die, but only one of those deaths seemed to me to be at all extraordinary. That was the death of my grandfather, William Leeper, who was an extraordinary man, exemplifying better than anyone I have known the capacity for unconditional love. I spent many hours at his bedside while he was dying and observed that on the day of his death an icy coldness gradually moved up his body until, when it reached his heart level, he died. Then, in the moment of his death, I saw a kind of shadowy substance that issued from the front of his body and moved up and away from him, very soon vanishing. Whatever had animated his body was gone, and it was clear that he was dead. I later observed other deaths, including those of my father and my mother, and I watched closely to try to observe what I had witnessed when my grandfather died. I have not witnessed that again, although I have heard accounts by others who reported observing what they took to be the soul departing from the body at the time of death.

The other deaths mentioned here are travelers' tales I only have heard, not personally witnessed. There are many such accounts, mostly from the East, and I cannot vouch for their authenticity. I am sure that William Welch observed something unique in his experience while attending the dying Gurdjieff, but whether that particular experience was mainly subjective or objective never will be known.

The greater our investment in the person who is dying— especially one who has demonstrated what we take to be extraordinary qualities and abilities—the less we may be able to accept that such a person could die an ordinary death. That said: the case remains open.

Chapter Thirty-one

Two Synchronicities

Carl Jung, the psychoanalyst who devoted much of his life to the study of the collective unconscious and to paranormal phenomena, was especially interested in what he called "synchronicities." A synchronicity consists of events that seem to be directly related, but that cannot be explained as examples of either psychological or physical causality as those are usually understood.

He gave as an example a patient who was describing to him a dream about a golden scarab, the scarab being a beetle sacred to the ancient Egyptians. There then appeared at the window a scarab-type beetle. Another example of this kind of synchronicity might be a clock that stops, or a favorite glass that shatters, at the time of its owner's death. The appearance of the actual beetle in Jung's example seems to go beyond the limits of ordinary coincidence. The two events appear to be connected by a potency of meaning that produces effects independent of objective causality.

Jung spoke of several categories of synchronicity. In the case of the scarabs, the events coincide in space and time, but are not causally connected within either category. A different kind of case is one where a person has detailed knowledge of something occurring at the same time, but elsewhere. A third kind of "acausal connection" is exemplified when a person has detailed knowledge of something which has not yet happened, but will happen in the future. It would seem that the second and third categories are quite different from the first. The case of the scarab beetle is, to me, of greater interest. It means that some force within a person can produce effects in the world outside the person. However, in the case of Jung's synchronicity, only certain kinds of effects can be produced, since a connection by *meaning* evidently must exist.

As Jung recognized, a synchronicity is most likely to occur when powerful symbols, and sometimes also strong emotions, are involved. The occurrence is more likely too, I believe, when the generating experience is of sufficiently prolonged duration.

Duration, intensity and potency of symbol or symbols—those factors brought together are gateways to powerful regions of Inner Space where symbols can generate effects in the external and objective world. Psychoanalysis sometimes fulfills the criteria and so may break down and through the always rather fragile boundaries between the normal and the paranormal. That breakthrough is of course an important objective of magic, shamanism and the authentic spiritual disciplines. Unlike psychoanalysis, however, these latter have elaborate methods for working with the phenomena made accessible once the breakthrough has occurred. The problem with magical and occult practices has never been that they do not work; rather, that they work unreliably, cannot be effectively regulated by laws, and too often are put to destructive uses. Their suppression also has seemed necessary to assure the supremacy of science. Despite all the efforts to discredit them, however, the fact remains that in most times and places magic, witchcraft and the like always have been practiced, and this would not be the case if they were only demanding exercises in futility.

One premise of magic always is that it can act upon the external world—affecting nature as well as human beings. The magician often works with the Gods and other nonhuman and superhuman beings. His or her work meets the criteria for bridging the worlds and generating paranormal phenomena—powerful symbols, duration and intensity. This definitely suggests that the *scientific* study of the experimental production of synchronicities is a real possibility.

If the conditions are provided, often the phenomena will appear whether wanted or not. The exploring Inner Space traveler seeking out the paranormal will almost certainly have encountered a rich variety of examples. In the case of synchronicities, I could provide several hundred cases at least, but will mention just a few where connections between the person and external events seem to go beyond any likelihood of just coincidence. They are especially striking examples, and will continue into my next chapter of travelers' tales.

In 1994, I commissioned a wood-carver and painter, Tom Strobel, to carve for me a standing seven-foot statue of the ancient Egyptian lioness-headed, human-bodied Goddess Sekhmet. He agreed to do this work at his studio in the Wisconsin woods, where he carved the figure from a single walnut log. I have had other artists make paintings and sculptures of the Goddess Sekhmet for me, and in each case I learned that the artist would go into a rather deep trance while working and would have a strong sense of Sekhmet's powerful presence.

Tom Strobel began the work out-of-doors but then, as the figure took shape, brought it into his studio, where he also lived and slept. He had once spent considerable time at a zoo where he became quite familiar with the sounds made by lions and tigers and other big cats. Now, when he would get ready to retire for the night, or just after retiring, he would hear what sounded to him like the roaring of a lion or some other big cat seeming to come from the woods just outside his house. Since he felt sure there was no lion in the woods, he could not decide whether these experiences were trance hallucinations or dreams, but he felt certain that they were related to his work on the lioness-headed figure of Sekhmet. Then, a couple of days before the statue was finished, he went out of his door in the morning and found on the door frame furrows in the wood that he thought could only have been made by some large cat. This experience was certainly not a dream, and he was sure that the furrows in the wood were absolutely and objectively real.

At the time, Tom Strobel also maintained a studio in Chicago, and he packed the statue on a truck and took it there to be crated and shipped to me in New York. Before leaving Wisconsin he had told some people at a nearby general store about hearing a big cat and then finding the claw marks on his door frame. They had all laughed and told him it was quite impossible. However, a day or so after his return, he received in the mail a clipping from a

Wisconsin newspaper sent to him by one of his farmer friends. It described a sighting not far from his studio of a large mountain lion and stated that no mountain lion had been seen in that area for a century. Synchronicity or mere coincidence?

In 1960, I was living in a small rural house in the Northwest Arkansas Ozarks near the White River. I had quit my job as a newspaper editor and had saved enough money to allow me to write undistracted for at least a year. I was working on a book that was published with the title *Eros and Evil—The Sexual Psychopathology of Witchcraft.* This was a book about medieval witch trials and especially accusations made against witches of entering into sexual relations with demons. I wanted to demonstrate how the hatred of matter, extended to a hatred of sex, had grown up within Christianity in a way that led to the witch trials and to anti-sexual morals and sexual pathologies still plaguing humankind.

Anyone familiar with this subject matter knows that it is extremely unpleasant and depressing. Several authors of histories of witchcraft have experienced severe clinical depression as a result of dealing with it. The accusations against witches, and the trials, truly disclose some of the darkest and most dismal reaches of the human psyche and soul. There are endless accounts of fiendish varieties of torture and execution, and even the intercourse with demons was sometimes described in so harrowing a way that one wondered how even inquisitors could bring themselves to suppose that witches would willingly yield to such experiences.

For example, a witch might be accused of having intercourse with a demon whose penis was covered with metallic scales. When he would have entered her, the scales would open out so that when he withdrew he would rip away the flesh from the interior of her vagina. Similarly, torture of witches—justified as needed to compel them to confess—might consist of skinning parts of the body, putting hot coals in the genitals, ripping off nipples with hot pliers, putting the witch in a so-called "iron maiden" so that many spikes penetrated her body, and so on. All of this was done, of course, in the Name of God and in order that goodness should prevail over evil.

For months I was immersed in thousands of pages of these materials as I organized and wrote my book. Witches were held to keep company with many of the most feared and hated of creatures—bats, poison toads, snakes, centipedes, tarantulas, scorpions and the like. Sometimes, it was said, around houses where witches lived, no grass but only poisonous weeds would grow, and trees sickened and died. There were strange storms and winds that also marked the dwelling place of a witch.

As I was writing this book, I began to experience a host of very unpleasant phenomena which really seemed to be intimately connected to what I was writing. My house and the area just around it were truly infested with scorpions and centipedes and tarantulas. I was friendly with some neighboring farmers and brought them to my house to show them this infestation and they were astonished. No one else in the area was experiencing anything similar. Several times when I got out of bed and went to my typewriter, I would find a scorpion sitting in my chair.

Outside the house, I found unusual numbers of dead birds and small animals. Several times, as I was walking the quarter-mile dirt road to my mailbox, I was almost struck by large dead limbs falling from the trees. The usually almost-empty creek bed near my house flooded several times, and bloated dead cows and semi-decayed pigs and goats floated past just a few feet from my door. While harder to authenticate, I noted that gusts of wind would seem to come out of nowhere, creating whirlpools of dust and looking like something one would be more likely to encounter in the desert. Overall, there was a kind of psychic pall that hung over the place, and friends who came to visit me during that time remarked in one way or another about the extremely oppressive feeling of the place—something never noted by them on previous visits.

Almost as soon as my book was completed, the whole array of phenomena vanished almost at once. In fact, after a few days there was not a single scorpion, centipede or other such creature to be found in my house, and although I remained there for another eight months or so, they never reappeared. Similarly, the oppressive psychic climate dissipated and everything returned to being as it had been before the writing of *Eros and Evil*.

I believe that this was a rather clearcut, complex and powerful example of mind—and possibly soul as well— interacting with nature. Or a case of synchronicity, as Jung would have it. Both the objective phenomena and the "feel" of the place, the psychic and emotional climate, were experienced by a number of other persons including the neighboring farmers, a newspaper editor, a philosopher and a psychologist who came to visit me at that time. I will next relate a series of events even more difficult—next to impossible, I'd say—for anyone not severely shackled by preconceptions about our reality and what is possible to regard as mere or simple coincidence.

Chapter Thirty-two

Straining Coincidence

In mid-March of 1984 I took up temporary residence on the Kona Coast of the Big Island of Hawaii. It had been arranged that I would do a ritual in the rather recently discovered cavern of the ancient Hawaiian Goddess Kapo. Participating with me in this would be a sacred dancer, an accomplished psychic, and a friend who had been introduced to the cavern by the young spelunkers who had found it. My friend had taken me, on a previous visit to Hawaii, to view what must be one of the most mysterious natural wonders of the world.

In Hawaiian mythology and religious tradition, Kapo is the Goddess of the Mauna Loa volcano on the Big Island, and her more famous sister, Pele, is the Goddess of the nearby Kilauea volcano. They have several other sisters, including Waka, Laka and Hi'iaka (Goddess of the sacred dance, or Hula).

On a famous occasion, in this tradition, a Pig God attempted to rape Kapo's little sister Waka. Kapo became aware of this and detached her own vagina, sending it flying towards a place near the island of Oahu where the Pig God was about to rape her sister. Kapo used the vagina to inspire so much lust in the Pig God that he forgot about her little sister and began to pursue the Kapo vagina. However, once Waka had escaped, Kapo eluded the would-be rapist and flew on to Oahu where she alighted on a rock, leaving the vagina's imprint. She then flew back to her home on the Big Island and hid the vagina in a cave that became a place of worship sacred to Kapo. Because of this episode, the Goddess became known as *Kapokohelele*, or "Kapo of the Traveling Vagina." In addition to this myth, there are legends about the sacred Kapo cavern and a vagina altar to be found in it where her high priests did their magico-religious work, worship and other practices including human sacrifice.

Few living persons believed the legends about the existence of this place until in the early 1980s it was actually found, or rediscovered. I was one of the first to visit the cavern, and I could scarcely believe my eyes when I first entered it. Created by the lava from Kapo's Mauna Loa Volcano, there is a vagina some thirteen feet in length and about seven feet in width with the labia folded back (Plate 7). In the center of the vagina there is a place for a human body to lie and meditate, or whatever Kapo's priests and priestesses may have done there. According to a gynecologist who examined it, it is the vagina of a woman who has had one child—consistent with Kapo as described in the mythology.

Just below and behind the vagina is a small naturally formed room with a kind of domed ceiling as if one were just to the rear of the vagina. This is known as Kapo's Womb Cave, and it was there I did the most important parts of the ritual.

Beyond the vagina altar, the cavern, formed by Kapo's lava, extends at least sixteen miles and remains unexplored by anyone now living. Just before the ground falls away into that space there is an area where at least one hundred phallic stones stand, also formed by the lava, and many of them resembling erect male sex organs with anatomical near-exactitude (Plate 8). They range in length from about one foot to three feet with appropriate circumference.

Off to the left of these upright phalli are a great many bones that have been determined to be those of old Hawaiian *ali'i*—nobility, royalty and probably high priests of the Goddess Kapo. Off to the right of the phalli, and about opposite from the remains just described, are more human bones, especially skulls. Many of these skulls have holes in them, and it was thought at first that this was evidence of holes made to relieve pressure on the brain, as that has been done by physicians throughout the world. More evidence, however, led to the conclusion that the holes in the skulls were for the purpose of extracting the brains of sacrificial victims and that the brains were eaten. The old Hawaiians believed that eating the flesh of a powerful person, and the brain in particular, would give the eater access to the *mana*, or power, of the one eaten. (It was for such a reason that the Hawaiians ate the famed explorer Captain Cook.)

Another physical feature of the cave is a hole in the roof of the cavern that could presumably be used by the vagina if it wanted to fly. The opening is much smaller than the vagina and, unlike other features of the cavern, appears to have been made by human hands. It was probably made by one of Kapo's priests, most likely to function as a light source.

It is appropriate here to remind the reader that while I am better known as a consciousness and human potentials researcher, neural and sensory reeducator, and sexologist, I have also spent many years in the study of magic, mythology and ancient religions. I especially have tried over decades to recreate a system of magic associated with the Egyptian Goddess Sekhmet and the Triad of Memphis (Sekhmet and the Gods Ptah and Nefer-tem). My book *The Goddess Sekhmet* describes some of what I have learned. I have also explored some of the magic associated with the Goddess Kali in India and the Goddess Hera in ancient Greece. These Goddesses, including Kapo, are all forms of the Great Mother. On the occasion of the ritual, I brought to Kapo special greetings from Sekhmet, Kali and Hera, and asked for some sign of recognition that the greetings were received.

The ritual at the sacred Kapo cavern was conducted on a Saturday afternoon, March 24, 1984. Early the next morning (Sunday, March 25) there occurred the first major eruption of Kapo's Mauna Loa Volcano to occur in almost half a century. Five days later, on March 30, Pele's Kilauea Volcano also erupted—the first simultaneous eruption with Mauna Loa since 1868, about 116 years previous to my ritual. That previous eruption was a legendary event which, of course, no one alive remembered, but which living Hawaiians had heard about from their grandparents and great-grandparents. In the legend, and in legends of Kapo, there were stories about fireballs streaking through the air. Now, well over a century later, there appeared great balls of fire hurtling back and forth between the Mauna Loa and Kilauea volcanoes.

Almost immediately after the first eruption, lava from Kilauea began advancing on the city of Hilo. Asked to take some action to save Hilo, the governor of Hawaii advised the native Hawaiians to pray.

In the ancient tradition, if a volcano erupts in response to religious or magical practices and the lava does no harm, then it means that the Goddess is pleasured and orgasmic. If, however, the lava is destructive, then it means that the Goddess is wrathful and has rejected, or is offended by, the work done.

In fact, at about the time when the great balls of fire started hurtling through the sky, and five days after Mauna Loa's original eruption, the lava stopped short of Hilo and was considered to have done only very minimal damage. This was taken by certain Hawaiian magicians as evidence that the Goddess was pleased.

Meanwhile, however, much was happening. Journalists from all over the world arrived on the Big Island to observe the spectacular phenomena. Many films and videotapes were made and are still readily available. It was an incredibly beautiful and awesome display of natural forces. While the lava was still advancing, and two days after the ritual at the cavern, I was scheduled to fly back home to New York. I wanted to stay in Hawaii, but finally yielded to the urging of my friends that I should leave. I was receiving threats of death curses and more material attacks by some native Hawaiian magicians, and my friends were afraid that they would come under attack if they continued to be associated with me. Even today, those friends who still live on the Big Island do not want to be named as having been involved in the Kapo ritual.

I left as scheduled, and when my plane was getting ready to land in New York, it was struck by lightning! The lightning did no harm, and it seemed to me like a kind of friendly good-bye caress from Kapo, who has power over all kinds of fire and lightning, not only the fires beneath the earth.

I wanted to have paintings of Kapo as *Kapokohelele* and of the sacred Kapo altar and cavern. When I asked my friend, the noted Hawaiian artist Herb Kane, if he knew of any, he said that none existed. He had done many paintings of Pele, but he thought that no Hawaiian artist would paint Kapo, and that included himself. A great taboo, he said, surrounds the Goddess Kapo.

In the aftermath of the eruptions, native Hawaiians persuaded the State of Hawaii to erect bars across the entrance to the cavern. They were afraid that the place would be vandalized or magically and religiously misused. I gather the Hawaiians presented both kinds of arguments to the State. "Undesirable elements" would be drawn to the site, on the one hand. On the other hand, there were those who feared that, in case of desecration, the full fury of the Goddess Kapo might be unleashed on the Big Island with tremendous destruction resulting.

So again the question arises as to which of two difficult positions to take: mere coincidence or some other explanation? Did the ritual done in this extremely strange and powerful place, involving an immensely potent symbol—archetype, or Goddess— trigger the event? Or did the extraordinary events that occurred just happen to coincide with the ritual and the appeal to the Goddess for a sign? If there were not so many other examples of "synchronicity" it would be easier to dismiss any causal or "acausal" connection.

Epilogue

The Millennial Opening of the Gates

It is clear from the reading of history based on contemporary accounts from many times and places that humans were never the only intelligent beings living on this planet. In ancient times, by numerous accounts, the Gods and the Goddesses interacted with humans, as did some very high beings known as Angels and Demons. In addition to that, there were all manner of lesser beings, written or told about in every time and place, and described as being quite real, not just mere fictions and fantasies.

The beings called Angels and Demons were next in rank to the Goddesses and Gods and were not regarded in the ways that we have come to think of them today. Demons, for example, were both "good" and "evil"—the ancient Greeks differentiated between those types as *Eudemons* and *Cacodemons*. It was the same with the Angels; they were both "good" and "bad"—not only in terms of their interactions with humans, but far more importantly, in terms of their relationships to Darkness and Light, Chaos and Order:

the War in Heaven.

All of these beings in very ancient times entered into all of the worlds accessible to humans, not even excluding the gross material world of the most ordinary and everyday reality. They did this, although the lower worlds are excremental to them, in order to perform certain actions with priests and magicians to try to enable human beings to awaken and rise above those lowest levels of the human reality. The attempt was not successful and the Gods withdrew, along with, for the most part, the Angels and Demons and other Higher Beings. For all but those specially trained to interact with the Gods, it became necessary to pray to an invisible Something presumed to exist in some Heaven, or to pay priests to do their talking for them.

Once the Higher Beings had gone, humans entered into all kinds of contracts and compacts with different lower beings, exchanging services of many kinds. One thinks of fairies, gnomes and imps, goblins and elves and incubi and succubi and gargoyles and all of the names that are given to such creatures in the various cultures and languages of the world. Many of these beings interacted sexually with humans for the pleasure of one or both parties. Those beings could also provide to humans such things as money and knowledge of future and distant events. Humans could provide safe places to stay, sometimes assist in the procurement of food, and also perform certain rituals and other actions to heal or empower or provide other benefits.

In addition to these lower entities—elemental spirits and the like—there were certain great beings manifesting as dragons, winged and other great serpents, gryphons, winged lions, unicorns, and sphynxes and others. These made themselves known for the most part only to magicians who knew how to summon and interact with them.

By the time of the Middle Ages in the West, but also throughout much of the world, all of these entities came under heavy attack from organized religions and from governments. They were branded as evil almost without exception, and those humans known to interact with them were accused of being in league with the Devil, trafficking with Demons, and the like, and were quite frequently subjected to very harsh punishments, including torture and death.

Since many of these nonhuman beings were not evil at all, and in fact were beneficent in almost every way, the attacks on them as evil caused them considerable distress. More, legions of priests, monks and nuns and other "religious" were assigned the task of unrelentingly seeking out such creatures and destroying them by means of certain chants and mantras and other sounds that, to those beings, were very often fatal, and which, in any case, caused them great torment.

Eventually, certain Higher Beings summoned to them some of the most advanced Magicians and spiritual Teachers from many places throughout the world, but especially from parts of Europe, Northern Africa and the Far East. At this very secret and Top Level Conference, still almost unheard of up until now, it was agreed that the lowest levels of the material reality would be left to human beings exclusively for five hundred years, or until the end of the Millennium in what the Christian world calls the year 2000. After that, according to the Contract, all of those beings that had once interacted freely with humans could do so once again.

While this Contract was never adhered to entirely, it was observed in the main, and interactions between human beings and intelligent nonhuman beings became rare. The Agreement was violated occasionally on both sides—on the human side mainly by occultists and witches, shamans, and a few other categories of persons exploring or working with lesser paranormals. Certain higher types of Magicians and Magician-Priests, whose Work involved interaction with very High Beings, even Gods and Goddesses, and who were importantly involved in the War in Heaven, were exempted from the Prohibition or Taboo. Such Magicians and Magician-Priests maintained contact, for example, as they always had done with Dragons, Sacred Serpents and a few others crucial to their work, especially as energy resources. In the East, the Most Holy Kundalini Serpent is recognized by the Tantrics to be a key figure in the great events marking the end of the Millennium just past and the start of the present one.

It was already apparent in recent decades that some of the old entities were jumping the gun, so to speak, and manifesting prematurely. The remarkable Magical Revival of the closing decades of the twentieth century could never have happened without the renewal of contacts between human and nonhuman beings. So, too, did the probably still more remarkable Goddess Reemergence testify to a premature breaking of the Contract, even by the Old Gods themselves.

The enormous proliferation of images of so many of the old nonhuman entities occurring in films in recent years testifies to unconscious responses to the breaches in the dimensional walls of consciousness through which these entities, once again, have been and are entering into the lower realms of matter and preparing mass renewals of the ancient interactions.

When, with the coming of the new Millennium, the Contract expired and the Gates Between the Worlds began to once again swing open, there started to occur a crisis of consciousness and a crisis of soul leading to a turning point of critical importance in the psychospiritual unfolding of humanity. The problems, more grave than as yet understood, which emerged in the year 2001, are a manifestation of this crisis of consciousness and crisis of soul. Information about the expiring of the Contract was deemed to be of such importance by one of the original Conferees, that news of it was "leaked," and the Secret Pact and the coming reopening of borders already had been made known in detail to carefully selected philosophers and magicians, as well as to the principal Teachers of the most important esoteric Schools.

We are at the threshold of times and events such as no one now living has experienced or perhaps is even able to imagine. But as one Saint I know well has reassured me: "There is probably no cause for excessive alarm about any of these admittedly quite remarkable goings-on. Our world will change, and change very greatly, and even fundamentally—not just in foreseeable ways, but mentally and spiritually in ways no one has been able to foresee. Nonetheless, knowledge of the probability, or even certainty, of a coming metamorphosis, is not a cause to be too fearful, but rather is a good reason to be extremely interested and curious. What is most reassuring, after all, is the definite fact that the Dragons are in charge" (Plate 9).

About the Author

Robert E.L. Masters has been, for more than three decades, director of research of *The Foundation for Mind Research*, which he cofounded with his wife Jean Houston. He is the author or coauthor of twenty-five books and more than one hundred papers and articles describing his research into the varieties of human behavior and potentials. His works have been translated into many languages, and he has taught and done research in Europe, Africa and Asia as well as the Americas.

He is recognized as a leading pioneer in consciousness research and the human potentials field. Dr. Masters has conducted on-site investigations of trance and psychoactive plant-induced altered states of consciousness in many different cultures and countries. He has pioneered applications of altered states in education and psychotherapy, as well as in neural, sensory and kinesthetic reeducation aimed at overcoming many different problems, but especially at making possible a larger and more productive access to human potentials.

Dr. Masters is a member of numerous professional, scientific and scholarly organizations including:

American Academy of Clinical Sexologists
American Psychological Association
American Psychotherapy Association
New York Academy of Sciences
Association for Humanistic Psychology

Robert Masters and his wife live in Ashland, Oregon.

Toxic Success:
How to Stop Striving and Start Thriving
by Paul Pearsall, Ph.D.
Foreword by Matt Biondi

Why America's Children Can't Think:
Creating Independent Minds for the 21st Century
by Peter Kline

Web Thinking:
Connecting, not Competing, for Success
by Dr. Linda Seger

The Initiation
by Donald Schnell
Foreword by Marilyn Diamond

Swimming Where Madmen Drown:
Travelers' Tales from Inner Space
by Robert Masters, Ph.D.
Foreword by Stanley Krippner